# ANCHOR BOOKS

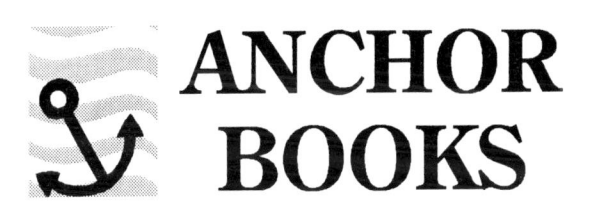

## *LINES OF LIFE*

Edited by

Heather Killingray

First published in Great Britain in 1997 by
ANCHOR BOOKS
1-2 Wainman Road, Woodston,
Peterborough, PE2 7BU
Telephone (01733) 230761

All Rights Reserved

*Copyright Contributors 1997*

HB ISBN 1 85930 556 3
SB ISBN 1 85930 551 2

# *Foreword*

Anchor Books is a small press, established in 1992, with the aim of promoting readable poetry to as wide an audience as possible.

We hope to establish an outlet for writers of poetry who may have struggled to see their work in print.

The poems presented here have been selected from many entries. Editing proved to be a difficult task and as the Editor, the final selection was mine.

Life is a strange thing; for as we journey through its many pitfalls and events - through the good times and the bad - and indeed, as we carry on continuously searching out the destiny it leads; we are often compelled to sit down, put pen to paper and just write. It could be about anything, maybe views on current affairs, a remembered moment or even someone we love. No matter what the subject, one of the best ways to express the feelings or views we have is often in the form of a poem or written verse.

Many people have done just that; as too have the talented authors within this book. Using their combined creative skills, together they offer you, the reader, over 140 very special poems to cherish and enjoy. So why not just read on and share along with them, some of their most favourite and very own lines of life.

I trust this selection will delight and please the authors and all those who enjoy reading poetry.

Heather Killingray
Editor

## CONTENTS

| | | |
|---|---|---|
| On the Umpteenth Wedding Anniversary | Brian Strowbridge | 1 |
| The Great Horizon | George Ponting | 1 |
| Election Day 1st May | Mary Elizabeth Murray | 2 |
| The Dolphin | Emily J Bloxidge | 2 |
| A Smile | Alexander Hamilton | 3 |
| Painful Attraction | Ronnie Bradshaw | 4 |
| Voyage | David Crossland | 4 |
| The Eternal Question | L Duncan | 5 |
| For A Bride | Liam Brophy | 5 |
| The Unbeliever | J D McKay | 6 |
| Ode To Dawn | R P H Fleming | 7 |
| When Lovers Dream Of Love | Gerald Aldred Judge | 7 |
| The River Foyle | John F McCartney | 8 |
| A Prisoner To His Love | Rosemarie Wood-Hall | 9 |
| My Endless Nights | Mary Birchall | 10 |
| Neighbours | Bridget Eyre | 10 |
| Bottoms Up! | Pauline Thomas | 11 |
| A Trip Along The River Teign | David Renshaw | 12 |
| In July | Anita Watts | 12 |
| My Lonely Walk Home | Sheila Climpson | 13 |
| Girl In A Pub | Gary Moran | 14 |
| Rain | J M Taylor | 14 |
| Witch | Stephen Denning | 15 |
| Sue Lawley's Hair | C Jacklin | 15 |
| Fred The Ted | Olive White | 16 |
| A Woman's Prerogative | R Young | 17 |
| Sharon | George Gallagher | 17 |
| Waterfall | Scott Haslam | 18 |
| Wobbly | Nick Purchase | 18 |
| I Will Always Miss You Grandad | Diana Sadig | 19 |
| Callers | Chris White | 20 |
| Frogs | M Taylor | 20 |
| Yorkshire Grit | Anthony Gibson | 21 |
| Mother | Indira Mohammed | 22 |

| | | |
|---|---|---|
| Flowerpot Magic | Bell Ferris | 22 |
| 1745 | D T Fletcher | 23 |
| Our Planet Earth | Mary Hulme | 24 |
| Lottery | Ivan Burton | 25 |
| The Death Of A Friend | J J S | 25 |
| Always - Hope | M Parnell | 26 |
| Hello Brother | Marjorie Horgan | 26 |
| Herbie | Julia Samson | 27 |
| Time Passes | J Wickens | 28 |
| Irish Magic | M Taylor | 28 |
| Foxy | S J Eley | 29 |
| My Canine Carer | Ria Blackwell | 30 |
| Misty Mountain Memories | Victor R A Day | 31 |
| Where I Belong | Irene Spencer | 32 |
| Untitled | Jason Barker | 32 |
| Time Passing | D Crossland | 33 |
| Death | R J Browning | 34 |
| The Rose | Marjorie May Johnson | 34 |
| Remember Christmas | Mark Tann | 35 |
| The Wonder Of Hearing | Ian Caughey | 36 |
| Childhood Years | C Langdon | 37 |
| Thank You For The Music | Pamela Evans | 38 |
| Silvery Fog | Carol Cecelia Olson | 39 |
| Carboot Sales | Dawn Moore | 39 |
| Guest Of Honour | Nigel W Briggs | 40 |
| The Other Woman | Jane Roberts | 41 |
| Journey Of A Soul? | Paul Roberts | 42 |
| Eyes | Mary Frances Mooney | 42 |
| On Emergence From Hibernation | Ian Barton | 43 |
| Holiday Time | Alwyn Jolley | 44 |
| Reasons To Be Cheerful | Ailsa Keen | 44 |
| Untitled | Sue Harper | 45 |
| Untitled | Matthew S Brierley | 45 |
| My True Love | Helen Abel | 46 |
| Start Again | R Muscroft | 46 |
| A Love I Have Loved | Francis Patrick Brown | 47 |
| The Spring | Celia Harper | 48 |

| | | |
|---|---|---|
| Strange Companion | Sandra Simpson | 49 |
| A Soldier's Fate | Hilary Ann Torrens | 50 |
| Gardening 1990-92 | Amber Gillmeister | 51 |
| Beauty In Poetry | Sandy Laird | 52 |
| Summer | A Usher | 52 |
| Jeremy | Sarah Barnes | 53 |
| Untitled | M Knights | 53 |
| Thoughts Of Springtime | Sue Strachan | 54 |
| Old Pendle | Valerie E Brown | 55 |
| Soldier's Wife | Helen Nelson | 56 |
| Nature's Grace | Tyron Allbright | 57 |
| Waste Of Space | Bob Lewis | 57 |
| Some Day | Betty Green | 58 |
| Does God Care? | J C Leadbeater | 58 |
| My Life Is Now Sold | Paul Warren | 59 |
| The Given Life | Ken Lowe | 60 |
| Leave Me Be | G E Khandelwal | 60 |
| Nearly There | J Knott | 61 |
| I Love You, Jesus | Paul Gainsford Bailey | 61 |
| True Happiness | Ian Davison | 62 |
| The Blue Silk Dress | Kellyanne Robertson | 63 |
| Oh Concrete One | Gary Parker | 64 |
| Free As A Bird | P D Dugdale | 65 |
| A Tribute To Mum | Margery Blake | 65 |
| Vestigial Drums | Theodore L Alder | 66 |
| Nightmares | Bethany Fowler | 67 |
| Humour | Lottie Bugler | 68 |
| Georgia | Helen Cronin | 68 |
| Music At The Creation Of Life, Fades With Death | Jennifer Polledri | 69 |
| The Dancer | P A Minson | 70 |
| Mother's Ruin | Kim Montia | 70 |
| Trash With Cash | Dennis Turner | 71 |
| To Dylan Thomas | Barbara King | 72 |
| The Pianists | Gwen Joselin | 73 |
| Mrs T | Linda Taylor | 74 |
| The Web Of Life | Lana J Povey | 74 |
| Our Future Peace | Michael Westlake | 75 |

| | | |
|---|---|---|
| The Reason | R P Scannell | 76 |
| Taking Our Food For Granted | Laura Keightley | 76 |
| Questions, Questions, Always Questions | J A Gray | 77 |
| The Odd Job Man | F J Groves | 78 |
| Harrogate | Ann Dulon | 79 |
| Interpreting | D I Bryden | 80 |
| Peace Of Mind | Lisa Corcoran | 81 |
| The Walk | Cheryl Mann | 82 |
| A Candle Burns | K Baiton | 83 |
| A Sobering Thought | N E Evans | 83 |
| The Wind | Marion Elvera | 84 |
| My Shepherd | R Wright | 84 |
| Remember Me | Deana Houghton | 85 |
| Wise Gambling | Lachlan Taylor | 86 |
| Autumn Morning | Ian Martin | 86 |
| Walking In The Rain With Man's Best Friend | Ian Barton | 87 |
| Labour's Victory | Stephanie Bones | 88 |
| The Ladybird | Alison Campbell | 88 |
| Prelude To Normandy | Sir MacGregor Fletcher | 89 |
| Election Fever May 1997 | Thelma Barnes | 90 |
| Silas Marner | Stephanie Fulfit | 91 |
| Untitled | Ann Thomas | 92 |
| Unfathomable Riches | Julie McKenzie | 93 |
| The New Image | Patricia Dickson | 94 |
| Seeking | Sylvia Lee | 95 |
| Embryo | Gary Parker | 95 |
| My Son | John Redmond | 96 |
| Poetry Is | F Gilpin | 97 |
| Silent Moon | Matthew Longfoot | 97 |
| The Jolly Boys' Outing | Adela Llewellyn | 98 |
| When Darkness Hits Reality | Paul Hallows | 99 |
| The Dancer | Marie Akers | 100 |
| Hymn For Youth | Margaret Haining | 101 |
| His Own World | Richard Clewlow | 102 |
| Trust | Kirsten Mason | 103 |
| Latchkey Days | Gillian McGimpsey | 104 |

| | | |
|---|---|---|
| Untitled | J Dunkley | 105 |
| Misty Memories And Clear Tomorrows | Jennifer Flint | 106 |
| Foreword | David Hazlett | 106 |
| Special Way | Coleen Bradshaw | 107 |
| England . . . | Dilip Datta | 108 |
| The Skiver | Chris Adamson | 109 |
| Off With His Head | John Urwin | 109 |
| Born For Better | R Middleton | 110 |
| The Woman Alone | Dorothy Thompson | 111 |

## On The Umpteenth Wedding Anniversary

Don't get excited, don't glow like a flame.
It's the same old thing all over again.

It's the same old words of love growing in the same old way

It's the same old cooking that welcomes me home each day.

It's the old faces with their same old smiles.
It's the same old helping hand helping me cover life's same old miles.

It's the same old sleepy grin that welcomes the morning tea.
It's the same old bald and tousled head, yes, it's the same old me.

It's the same old appreciation, what else is there to say?
It's the same old everything that grows and grows each day.

So don't let's get excited. Don't let's make a fuss.
'Cos, it's the same old, same old same,
Well, it's us.

*Brian Strowbridge*


## The Great Horizon

There must be other lands,
Beyond the great horizon;
There must be other souls,
With a greater understanding:

Perhaps some day I'll find
Them;
Beyond the great horizon.

Lingering in its mystery,
Is a peace I do not know;
A world of calm serenity;
Peaceful as a blue lagoon;
Quiet as the moonlight glow.

*George Ponting*

## ELECTION DAY 1ST MAY

The day dawned warm and sunny as if to herald a new era,
Election Day, the 1st of May,
There seemed a buzz of excitement through the land,
A Labour victory seemed sound,
We must wait till evening and later still,
Before we can see our hopes fulfilled.

The results came thick and fast,
Our hopes seemed reality at last,
Cheers and victory and celebration,
Lights in many houses, people waiting and many
Hoping for a Labour jubilation.

There is a fresh new breeze blowing through the land,
We hope that fate deals a fairer hand,
New hopes, aspirations and a great new way of thinking.
The fires have been lit to inspire the flame of hope,
Hopes for a better way of living.

*Mary Elizabeth Murray*

## THE DOLPHIN

The dolphin swimming freely,
Is startled by a boat.
It now is diving downwards,
As once it was afloat.

It knows the awful sound,
The fishing trawler makes.
It hides in desperation,
Its poor old bones they shake.

Mother told *this* dolphin,
To always be aware,
Of the wicked and hurtful people,
Ruling land up there.

But poor old dolphin David,
Was not taught this rule.
He now pays the price,
Of men who are hurtful and cruel.

***Emily J Bloxidge (14)***


## A SMILE

It doesn't cost a fortune;
And can't be bought or sold:
To the ill-fated in this unjust world;
Worth more than jewels or gold.
The well-to-do can't buy it;
No matter what their wealth;
But each of us can share it;
With happiness and health.
You'll never see it in the shops;
Although it's widely sought;
People search for it every day;
But still it can't be bought.
It has no commercial value;
And cannot be assessed;
Each person that exists on earth;
With its potency is blessed.
To radiate its magic power;
If only for a while;
Each day we live, it's ours to give;
A warm and tender *smile*.

***Alexander Hamilton***

## PAINFUL ATTRACTION

We have tools for this and tools for that,
Some we don't use, but like to look at,
We have saws and drills, sockets and spanners,
But the best all-rounder has to be hammers.

Balanced to perfection, made of forged steel,
The sound of one striking has a musical appeal.
The problem with hammers - for reasons unknown,
Are attracted to thumbs and let it be known.

It must be the shape they view as a threat,
And try to deform; the first chance they get.
We have all cracked our thumbs when sinking a nail,
We shout, swear and curse or practise the scale.

I once asked a joiner the best way to miss them,
He said, 'All I can tell you is the best place to hit them!'

*Ronnie Bradshaw*


## VOYAGE

round wooden explorer boat
outstare both storms and calms afloat
sailing oceans myself crew alone
anchor deep off paradise home.
fragrant winds, spices, golden lands
tidal waves white virgin sands,
lantern cabin dim guiding light
compass, sextant, orbiting satellite,
wonder stare at timeless monuments
following stars to polar continents,
and when safe harbour final come
know myself because myself i won;
from sofa-wreckage dreaming i awake
by many calculations did miscalculate.

*David Crossland*

## THE ETERNAL QUESTION

Thought? What is this strange thing we call thought?
For the hidden answer, wise men have sought,
Is it a fusion of untold dreams
With far-off memories, distant screams
Of pleasure, sadness, love and hate,
Of poverty, while men sit and wait
For food and water, riches galore,
This *thought* goes on forever more,
Prehistoric man, he had to think
What food to eat, what juice to drink,
But unlike man, thought has not evolved.
The puzzle I speak of remains unsolved,
Men wrestled with theories, against ideas they fought,
Can anyone tell me in truth, what is thought?

*L Duncan (12)*


## FOR A BRIDE

Life's water's changed to Cana wine, and now
Obscures the memory of insipid days;
The past is drowned in the delirious draught
Of wondrous wine made at a whispered vow
Of flushing lives merging as gaze meets gaze
While love's new consecrated cup is quaffed.

Life's charged with sacred purpose now: no hour
Hangs listless on time's string, but is a bead
In the repeated round of prayer, the years
Will lag no longer, but will gather power
From lives close-linked and shared, and love will lead
Out of the shadows of forgotten fears.

*Liam Brophy*

## THE UNBELIEVER

'I don't believe in ghosts' he said
As he climbed the stairs.
'It's Hallowe'en' came the reply,
'Not the night to go to your bed
Without a prayer.'

His laughter floated down
To the listener below.
But hush, was that an echo,
Or had someone else joined the jest?

He lay in bed and chuckled again.
The clock struck the witching hour.
Someone was watching: waiting.

His chuckle became a cackle
As his teeth clicked like castanets.
The floorboards creaked.
The window flew open.
The bedclothes slid to the floor.

His screams froze in his throat.
Slowly the hour passed; s o  s l o w l y.

His hands clutched back the bedclothes.
As warmth returned, he crossed the room,
Closed the window and locked the door.

'I still don't believe in ghosts'
He said, as he climbed back into bed . . .
'Don't you?' asked a voice, like the
Whisper of dead leaves.
'Then, who is this by your side?
Like you, those draughts, I can't abide.
So, till next Hallowe'en, I am your fiend!'

*J D McKay*

## ODE TO DAWN

I sat this morning on the lawn,
To watch the coming of the dawn,
The sunlight spilling o'er the tiles,
It had travelled, miles and miles.

The birds were singing in the trees,
Their lovely plaintive melodies,
The squirrels running everywhere,
Seemingly without a care.

Blackbirds singing on the bough,
And the doves and pigeons cooing now,
Great tits, long-tailed tits, and blue tits so small,
They are all building their nests in the nest boxes so tall.

God's chosen people came to the door,
Who are you? And what do you want, anymore?
What they want, is a lot more cash,
How will they spend it? On even more trash.

**R P H Fleming**


## WHEN LOVERS DREAM OF LOVE
*(For Sally)*

I thought perchance I heard a nightingale
  singing from above,
upon this day of sweet romance
  when lovers dream of love.

And there for a moment
  when the moment met its goal,
I closed my eyes and you were there
  your smile fluttered in my soul.

**Gerald Aldred Judge**

## THE RIVER FOYLE

Flowing wide 'twixt Derry banks
Dark tidal rush unfurling;
Farms nestle green along its flanks
A river vast with deep-set swirling.

Clouded with suspended mud
Reflected blue from azure sky;
In bygone days so prone to flood
Seagulls swoop and steal and cry.

From Faughan mouth to Lifford bridge
A river famed for fish;
In summer high so plagued with midge
Each salmon runs to gravel niche.

Whose water witnessed Viking raids
And bore the boats of Columkille;
The curdling cries and Norsemen blades
Chilled clerics' hand with quivering quill.

Down through the siege of eighty-nine
The cannons roared and spat;
The riverside was the firing line
But Derry walls stood round and fat.

Now ships no longer berth and stay
The Glasgow boat is time forgot;
The empty wharves are a parking bay
And cars replaced the sailing yacht.

So flow you torrent of renown
Fair maiden city on your banks;
Culmore, Killea, and every town
A river high in history's ranks.

***John F McCartney***

# A Prisoner To His Love

Dear Rosemarie,
        And howfore is the princess of that
jewel, within my night.
For the star of your sweet love
Shines your heart's desire so bright.
Oh but to hold you, to hold you so close to me
As I softly whisper in your ear
Ah yes, my sweet Marie
And as I kiss you tender, my blood
              races at the thought.
For the passion like a fire
From the flames, that love has caught
As you lead me slowly, through those
              pleasures of your heart.
The inner realms of rising tides
Like our physical loving begins to start
The rainbow, will descend, as those hot
              kisses fall like rain.
The night shall fade from us
But the pleasures will remain.
So if you awake from a dream
Raven wing beats in the air
Then you'll know, my petite princess
That when it mattered, I was there.

***Rosemarie Wood-Hall***

## MY ENDLESS NIGHTS

The day is done, mum's gone to bed
For me there's another long night ahead.
The hands on the clock seem to crawl around
As I sit and listen for the slightest sound
Night after night it's always the same
Mum's up and down it seems like a game
Then she settles down and I watch TV
My only company myself and me
I need some distraction so I make some tea
And gaze through the window but there's nothing to see
There's only darkness, there's no-one around
I go back to listening for the slightest sound
Is that mum up again? I'll just go and see
Yes it was mum so glad to see me
A trip to the bathroom, then back into bed
'Goodnight, God bless love' that's what she said
Well another night's over, I'll turn out the lights
This is the sadness of all of my nights.

*Mary Birchall*


## NEIGHBOURS

I tell you girl she's as common as muck
Doesn't know her do's from her don'ts
Mix with her and you won't get much luck
With all of her wills and her wont's.

They say that her washing could do with a boil
And the garden's a positive tip
Her husband's neck is as black as the soil
And her lad has got far too much lip.

Watch out she's coming, give her a smile
It's good to see you, how long will it be
It must be many a while
The kettle's on come in for some tea.

*Bridget Eyre*


## BOTTOMS UP!

My wife doesn't half make me frown
When she opens her crisps upside down!
This inverting the pack
Is an unconscious knack -
I'm convinced she's not playing the clown!

And I've found there are certain key flavours,
Like beef, and the kind she most savours -
Those spicy corn snacks
In the six or twelve packs -
That this frequent phenomenon favours!

So I've drawn up a plan - I'll run through it:
Take one pack of crisps - nothing to it!
Now, ere she can spot 'em,
I'll open the bottom,
And then, why, I'll just . . . Superglue it!

Well, now I am rather downcast!
In the short space of time that has passed,
My plan's proved a flop,
For she's opened the top . . .
As *my* thumb to the bottom's stuck fast!

*Pauline Thomas*

## A Trip Along The River Teign

A trip we did arrange to go along the River Teign,
What lovely scenery there is to be seen.
People they gave us a smile and a wave,
The Teign is so calm you need not be brave.
We saw a family of swans and plenty of seagulls too,
And also in the sky the terns as they flew.
Now and again a train would go by speeding along the track,
Taking passengers from city to city, they travel there and back.
As we went on this enjoyable ride we saw the different types of rock,
It was in the early evening so it was very quiet at the dock.
The crew took us as far as they could go and then we did stop,
All kinds of food for us to eat and plenty of drink mainly pop.
Time was moving on and it was getting dark,
In the distance you could hear a dog bark.
There is a pub we passed where you can have a drink or a meal,
And you can get a very reasonable deal.
As we went under Shaldon bridge the crew had to lower the mast,
What I did enjoy was the fact we did not go very fast.
A couple of ships came into the docks to be loaded up with clay,
I am just glad that we did not get in their way.
A very interesting evening we have had and there was no rain,
I am sure that one day we will do this pleasant trip again.

*David Renshaw*


## In July

In July it'll be just you and I
No more unhappiness
Blues or cries
I am free from the attachments
That seem to bind me
In our separate lives

In July the dream becomes real
We live together
Express the love we feel
I am holding on to you
Into the world we sail.

*Anita Watts*


## MY LONELY WALK HOME

I walked through a graveyard, late one night
When I heard a funny noise, and got an awful fright.

The shadows they were short, the shadows they were long
A church bell started ringing, with a big loud bong.

I was taking a short cut, so I could get home quick
But I got so scared and frightened, I felt quite sick.

I saw something moving, behind a large gravestone
It looked tall and skinny, just like a body made of bone.

The head it moved from side to side, the arms waved in the breeze
But it was only a shadow, made by moonshine through the trees.

I had half a mile to go, the graveyard it was long
So I quickened up my pace, and as I went I sang a song.

I am not frightened, and scared I will not be
If there are any ghosts about, they won't get me.

In the morning when I woke up, my hair had gone quite grey
So the next time I went out, I came home a different way.

*Sheila Climpson*

## Girl In A Pub

No drink, no think
Too intense, too talkative.

Distance and near,
Plenty of fear for her bit of gear.

Drunken, disorderly
Shabby, sometimes flabby.

Eze please, allow for her squeeze,
For you and I know she is only a pricktease.

Open, closed, free and red blooded.
Gagging to be manipulated.

Cute and all show,
All talk but under the influence no healthy flow.

I want that girl in the pub to go
For she feels no place unless she is below.

**Gary Moran**


## Rain

A rainy day
What more to say?
It's Bank Holiday
What will tomorrow bring?
Maybe a touch of spring
Bright sun cold wind
Summer's on its way
Will be here some day.

**J M Taylor**

## WITCH

A smell of sulphur from a passing witch
Scouring hedgerow, verge, and ditch.
She knows the virtue of herb and flower
Added to spells in the witching hour.
Hemlock and nightshade, a twig of yew
Plants of poison, 'tis so true.
Her craft she knows so very well
Secrets of it she'll never tell.
Power of nettle, root or weed
She claims they work very well indeed.
Some respect, some hold a fear
Never approaching this haggard old dear.
A vision in black in the deep of a wood
Speaking in tongues beneath a pointed hood.
If you should meet, never look her in the eye
They say your soul, she'll try to buy.

*Stephen Denning*


## SUE LAWLEY'S HAIR

I'm looking at Sue Lawley's hair,
Roche moutonnée quiffing flair.
Ragged right, smoothing left,
Parting set in locking cleft.
Crisp an sugar crystal set,
Skiing ruts and slalomettes.
Hotting lights dulled to grey,
Inning upping swillow hay.
Fixing eyes now lowering dare,
To meet the eyes beneath the hair.

*C Jacklin*

## FRED THE TED

I am a little teddy bear, sitting on a bed
My master's name is Luke, and my name is Fred.

My leg it has gone missing, and my arm hangs by a thread
And I've only got one eyeball, in my poor old head.

I'm taken down to breakfast, then off we go to play
We're also going to the park, as it's a lovely sunny day.

We go upon the swings, the roundabouts and slides
I think I feel a wee bit sick, with all these bumpy rides.

One ear has split in half now, and my stuffing's coming out
Luke notices and cuddles me, then gives a great big shout.

He goes and shows me to his mum, who takes me with a frown
She sets to work upon my leg, but it's put on upside down.

My arm is placed upon my shoulder, almost on my neck
Oh dear, next comes my ear, I must look quite a wreck.

This is sewn on by my nose, I do feel awfully funny
The eye's replaced with a great big button, Oh you silly mummy.

My body's rather crooked, now my bits have been sewn back
I was really very worried, in case I was put in the rubbish sack.

But Luke is pleased and picks me up, I get another cuddle
He loves me very much you see, even though I look a muddle.

So with all the love that I am given, by Luke who's nearly seven,
I'm such a lucky teddy bear, I think this must be heaven.

**Olive White**

## A WOMAN'S PREROGATIVE

So, who needs a man -
I used to think, not me!
But over the years of loneliness
And domesticity
I've come to the conclusion
That they're good to have around
When you can't afford a tradesman
For the problem that you've found -
Like the drawer that will not open
Or the window that won't shut,
Or to help you with the plaster
On the finger that you've cut.
And then, there is the spider -
He's been sitting there all week -
I suspect he must be very dead
Or very, very meek!
And other complications
Like the blocked extractor fan -
Yes, I've changed my mind completely
And I wish I had a man . . .

*R Young*


## SHARON

With your long blond
Hair and blue eyes
Your cute smile I
Fell in love with you.
I love you so much
It hurts. I pray
That one day you will
Love me as well.

*George Gallagher*

## WATERFALL

I can see the waterfall gushing to the ground,
The water flows away nowhere to be found,
The waterfall is gushing and crashing,
It is plunging and clashing.

The waterfall is very high,
It reaches up to touch the sky,
The water sprays and hits my face,
I run to find a hiding place,

As I quickly peer,
I decide not to go too near,
Soon I get up and go,
Not going too near though,

The water bashes to the river,
When I see it, it give me quite a quiver,
I like the sight of the water cascading down,
It is the king of the river without a crown.

*Scott Haslam (10)*


## WOBBLY

There was once a man
Who lived in a bubble,
What you often find
In his bewildered mind
Is obbly wobbly trouble.

His dinner was tasty,
Insect salty soup.
Hopping like rabbits
Were his hopes and habits,
They danced in a group.

Two cats courting
On the riverbank wall;
The owl toots
To the outburst of
Violins and flutes
While another folds
To make himself small.

*Nick Purchase*


## I WILL ALWAYS MISS YOU GRANDAD

Grandad grandad come back to me
I love you so much and your death hurts me.
Remember when I was young
I used to be your beloved one.

My birthday came you weren't there
No presents for me, it seems unfair.
Grandad you were my light for the day and night
My song my talk my hour my midnight.

My world torn apart without a man like you
My hopes and dreams that I had about you
Are all gone just like the others too.

I will always miss you grandad with tears
Coming down my eyes
With hurt in my heart that I can never hide.

Come back grandad for my sake and yours
There are no words for me without your words.

*Diana Sadig*

## CALLERS

Fifty thousand salesmen
Knocking on your door.
Selling double glazing
Like they've never done before.
Do you want a catalogue?
Do you want a kitchen?
Do you want your lawn mown?
Are your hedges overgrown?
Do you want a newspaper?
Can you pay your milk?
I will clean your windows
With a rag as soft as silk.
And when you've seen them all off.
The doorbell starts to ring.
It's the end of the year carols
Children come to sing.
When we want some peace and quiet.
Our privacy protected
Let's put our feet up
And have the doorbell disconnected.

**Chris White**


## FROGS

I like my frogs
Better than dogs
They sit on my shelf
Some like myself
Some old
Some cold
Some dangle legs
None produce eggs.

**M Taylor**

## YORKSHIRE GRIT

A contrast around every corner,
In Yorkshire you're sure to find
Lots of factories and chimneys.
With a backcloth spread behind
- of rolling hills and scenery
Fit to blow the mind
Yorkshire's a colourful county
Filled with colourful people you'll find.

Huddersfield produced a Prime Minister
Harold Wilson by name
Anita Lonsborough and Roy Castle
All add to Huddersfield's fame.
But then again in the present day
Order must prevail
Dewsbury's Betty Boothroyd is a match for any male.
Order! Order! You hear her shout
That quietens them down and sorts them out.

In Yorkshire a shovel is never a spade
Things are seen for what they are.
The beautifully formed countryside
Stretches from near to far
It's wonderful! It's miraculous
It's so naturally displayed
All this and more was made by God
So majestically, so grand
It couldn't be the product
Of a fickle human hand.

***Anthony Gibson***

## MOTHER

We will never forget you
We shall never be apart
Even though you were taken from us
Safely you are held in our hearts.

Simply the way you smiled at us
Simply the way you cared
Always the way you held us
Unconditional love you shared.

Softly you'd take our hand
Always managing to understand
You'd hold us close, kiss our worries away
Tell us that you loved us every day.

No other mother loved more than you
No other friend to us so true
No other memory of you so bright
You will always remain part of our lives.

**Indira Mohammed**




## FLOWERPOT MAGIC

There's a sunflower in my garden
That has grown to five foot ten
It reminded me of 'Little Weed'
Friend of the Flowerpot Men

My children used to love them
And still remember to this day
How they double-talked to 'Little Weed'
In their funny flowerpot way

So I sorted pots out from the shed
Then threaded them with twine
Painted names on flowerpot hats
And straw hair does just fine

Now, fast regaining their lost fame
As children call to see
Bill and Ben the Flowerpot Men
Recalled from history.

***Bell Ferris***

## 1745

From the forests, and the glens, the isles and the braes, on Culloden
field met Charlie's men Cumberland's cruel cannon play,
stood they fast before his might, wind and sleet in their face.
Highland broad sword out for the fight, as Cumberland's cannon
quickened pace.
But no word came from Charlie's lips to break the enemy's stance, as
ball and shot, cut through the lines, and thinned the tartened ranks.
In mounting anger, they begged their chief's advance, but got no reply
some clans then broke their line, and charged at Cumberland's flank.
Poor Charlie's fortune had altered course, as Cumberland butchered
those not dead.
Till Charlie saw that there was little left of his Highland force, and on
advice mounted horse and fled.
On Culloden field you can hear on the wind the sound of weeping
As Prince Charlie's ghostly tears fall on the graves of his highland men
asleeping.

***D T Fletcher***

## Our Planet Earth

Wherever man has trod
Destruction follows him
Nature takes the biggest toll
Trees ripped from limb and limb

We must not find new places
For in some short-lived years
A wilderness will follow
Our earth has swallowed fears

God gave our earth in trust
For man to love and praise
But savage use of nature
Has brought destructive ways

We must not spread this horror
It's like a sickening plague
'Cos man won't learn a lesson
For he will rant and rage

I do not see an answer
But this I surely know
Don't let mankind to settle
On planets pure as snow

All nature on our planet
Can't follow, cannot flow
From man's destructive hand-print
If man's allowed to go.

**Mary Hulme**

## LOTTERY

At eight-o-five, our house comes alive.
We gather around, and turn up the sound,
To see the balls roll.
There's just forty-nine; only six need be mine,
Or five in a row, if the bonus ball shows,
To make our lives whole.

It's harmless fun, when the week's work is done,
To help a good cause, and fixed by the laws,
Make them money.
A variety show, see that Lancelot go!
Self-satisfied beam on Bob's face, so clean,
Like it really was funny.

It's no longer a lark, when we sit in the dark.
No cash to be found, for they've had the last pound
Of our Income Support.
And isn't it sad, that the best chance we had
In a life full of falls, was a load of old balls,
Our last resort?

*Ivan Burton*


## THE DEATH OF A FRIEND

I can't believe she is no more,
my lovely young neighbour from next door
Almost home when a speeding car hit hers head on
and now that sweet young girl has gone.
I can't believe that gentle Beth
has so prematurely met her death.

*J J S*

## Always - Hope

If feeling weary
      Of daily life,
Sad from sorrow, or troubled strife
Ask the Lord, 'for a helping hand'.
You don't have a magic wand,
When 'all alone', help you seek.
But a little prayer,
      To ask for help
For guidance, from the stress we bear.
Knowing he is always there,
      To help us,
When all seems bleak
The long dark tunnel
He will, help us through
So in your prayers,
      When 'things' come right
Thank the Lord,
      For his guiding light.

*M Parnell*

## Hello Brother

When you go out walking through the town
and someone is begging don't look down,
don't pass them by like you could not care
and remember your manners it's rude to stare.

Just stop and think could be you or yours
you have yet to come up against closed doors,
now is the time to take stock and to bother
you say you're a Christian? Well there is your brother.

He won't expect you to understand
but the least you can do is to offer a hand,
just a few pence to buy him a meal
come on be that Christian it's no big deal.

*Marjorie Horgan*

# HERBIE

Herbie has a lovely head
Like a tiger it's been said
With well-planned stripes on face and cheeks,
Black, over gold, and grey in streaks.

A darkest tabby he's been called,
With thick black stripe between his ears
And down his back towards his tail
Which stands up straight so he can flail.

His name is Herbert but he feels
This has a cissy seal
So now the name that's his when called
Is 'Herbie'; and he's far from bald;

In fact if you should turn him over,
You will find he's white all over
Under chin and all the way
To four white feet, just slightly splay.

But in his golden eyes displayed
The central core is black and rayed
And gleams, as though through thickest jungle,
As he purrs his rumble mumble.

*Julia Samson*

## TIME PASSES

It seems when you get up in the mornings
It's time to go to bed at night
Time rushes by so quickly
No sooner it's dark than it's light
I sometimes wish time would stand still
When I see the lines on my face and grey hair
Time goes more slowly for some folk
It's one thing in life that's not fair
At least there's one consolation
An excuse can be used with this line
When asked for help you can answer
'I would but I haven't the time!'

*J Wickens*


## IRISH MAGIC

A little man sat beside the road
he wore a funny hat we had a little basket
filled with this and that
a pair of silly laces and a funny little mat
a length of pretty ribbon a small collar for a cat,
He was eating bread and cheese just enough
to last the day,
he was there this very minute now he has vanished
right away.
Then I saw a little lady on a tiny fairy bike
she looked around and called a name
then disappeared from sight.

*M Taylor*

## Foxy

Blissfully sleeping, doing no harm
Here comes the storm, erupting the calm
Louder and louder, death draws near
The aim of the exercise, precisely clear.

The hounds in a frenzy
As they follow the scent
They've nearly found him
Time is now lent.

He bolts like a racehorse
Adrenaline flows
Too late someone's seen him
And shouts 'There he goes'

Through fields, over hedges
He runs for his life
His eyes are focused
He's sharp as a knife.

Reality is a cruel race
Death is behind him
At a frightening pace
He cannot give up, the going's too tough
The frenzy is quickening
This game is too rough

Poor foxy is tiring
He's dripping with sweat
His heart palpitating
At the sight he has met

He's given up now, and dropped to the floor
The hounds surround him, bloodthirsty for more
As he sees his last vision, he lays on his back
Before the huntsman cried 'Attack boys attack.'

*S J Eley*

## My Canine Carer

My friend does not talk
but walks with me
you have to experience it,
to know and to see.

My friend walks on four,
alongside my two
her grammar is poor,
but she gets me through.

My friend snuggles up to me
loving and kind,
in our time together
our hearts were entwined.

My friend is canine
for me she did care,
in all our time
she made life feel fair.

My friend, my guardian,
she grew up with me
nothing like her,
any other breed could be.

Even though she could not speak
no-one could match our years
with our own special communication,
we blasted our fears
now I am left alone,
to cope with the tears
goodbye my friend,
we shall seek comfort from our peers.

The time has come
for my friend to say goodbye,
she's gone to the land
of loving canines in the sky.

I think you will understand
yes I think you will see,
she was canine
but she cared for me.

*Ria Blackwell*


## MISTY MOUNTAIN MEMORIES

The mist laid heavy on the snow covered hills
the sky was brilliant red,
the air was so cold upon that day
causing pain within our heads.

With a tear in our eye we thought we would die
as we walked that final mile,
and then into sight came a front porch light
which gave a warning smile.

We started to pray as we headed that way
through snow some four foot deep,
into a warm and cosy room
where we did fall asleep.

The morning light blocked out the night
no footprints could I see,
coming from the mountain side
made by my friend and me.

The snow lay crisp and sparkling
the trees shuddered in the cold,
jolting memories of the night before
which my mind would always hold.

*Victor R A Day*

## WHERE I BELONG

I look down from a hillside, as dusk begins to fall.
Below me lies my hometown, the place I love best of all.
The chimney stacks, not so ugly now, mellowed against darkening sky
Down there are all my memories, grown fainter as times gone by.
The park where we played as children - is bathed in evening mist
And I can only vaguely make out the oak tree where we first kissed
The football field where our voices rang - for goals that were
                                                    never scored
The cinema closed and decaying now - a retreat when we got bored
The church where we were married, not grand enough to sport a spire
The place where we swapped our cigarette cards - while
                                            practising for the choir
And as the darkness deepens it's as if night has drawn a veil
Over shabbiness I *don't* remember - it's a long time since I hit the trail
And now one by one the lights come on, a fairy chain twinkling bright
It makes a pretty picture - imperfection hidden by night.
A far cry from the neons of Manhattan - where night is as bright as day.
But tonight I am oh so happy - because I have come home to stay.

*Irene Spencer*




## UNTITLED

Frosty nights and rainy days
red hot sunshine, summer haze
chilling winds, scattered rain

Good old England, it never ends,
the same old weather again and again,
a fertile country full of green, the likes
of which you've never seen.

Buckingham Palace has a queen
the Tower Bridge has jewels that gleam,
at Nelson's Column we play again, the same
old England, it never ends.

*Jason Barker*


## TIME PASSING

friends there is none anymore
everywhere you go
        you've been there twice before,

horizons gone before your eyes
all you ever dreamed
        awakening into lies,

days' blank pages in a book
landmarks torn-down
        everywhere you look,

family counted on one hand
hallway mirror
        framing one-man band,

telephone expectant waiting
growing insecure
        afternoon horse-racing,

library news whispering browsing
censorious stare
        authority frowning,

walking ugly terraced street
know nobody
        who you never meet.

*D Crossland*

## DEATH

Death is so very lively
Dancing from life to life
Its appearance so seldom timely
Too soon too late its favourite wife

It cares not who or what you are
Infant child or worldly star
For if you attract its gleaming eye
Expect soon to bid this world goodbye

To wonder as to how it does choose
The pressed gangs crews for the eternal cruise
By compassion or mercy not I'll wager
More a random pick from its fateful ledger

So live your life as you would wish
Be rich or poor be false or true
For all too soon on that fateful page
Its hand will fall your name to pick
His ship to crew

***R J Browning***

## THE ROSE

The rose it swayed before me
As gentle as a breeze,
It seemed to say 'Look again'
God gave you eyes to see.

I looked upon its beauty
And my heart it filled with pride,
But sadness was in my heart that day
So I just stood there and cried.

Through my tears I looked more close
And on that rose a tear of dew,
The rose, it seemed to say 'Don't cry'
Just let me cry for you.

*Marjorie May Johnson*


## REMEMBER CHRISTMAS

Merry Christmas
Happy New Year
Singing Lang Syne
Knocking back beer
Jolly fat Santa, lots of good cheer
Children out playing, in cold wind or snow
Fingers all numb, faces that glow
High wind chill factor
Three feet of snow

Silly hats, crackers don't bang
Over-full bellies, braces may twang
Christmas pud alight with the brandy
Children sing songs
And rot teeth on candy

Children get up
At first crack of dawn
To build up their snowmen
On their front garden lawn
Buttons for eyes, a carrot for nose
A scarf round his neck
And daddy's old clothes

*Mark Tann*

# THE WONDER OF HEARING

I asked a simple question, as I arrived by her side,
Soon wondering why it was she had never replied,
Until I learned of one precious sense she was sadly bereft
As her companion explained - 'Claire is profoundly deaf;'
And I later pondered our hearing - the joy that it brings
Through our appreciation of just so many things
That this young girl to savour may too dearly have wanted,
But yet which I confess I had oft taken for granted -
The sweetness of birdsong, high amongst the trees;
The gentle whisper of a cooling summer breeze;
The alarm clock's shrill ring, getting us up with the lark;
The cat's 'thank you' purr, and the dog's warning bark;
The companionship radio can bring when alone;
And conversing with friends and loved ones on the telephone;
Or just hearing those wonderful three words 'I love you' -
That simple phrase which brings joy like none other can do.
And there is music's mighty power to leave the emotions stirred;
The new-born baby's first cry, then later its first word,
And that inexplicable feeling, for the parents, sublime,
On hearing 'Mama' or 'Daddy' for the very first time.
And for our safety and well-being this sense's value is clear,
As announcements of importance we can instantly hear,
For instruction plus warning the listening ear receives,
Shaping so much that the intellect knows, accepts and believes.
Is not this sense to our hearts therefore all the more endearing
As we comprehend fully the true wonder of hearing,
Surely making us thankful to our heavenly Father above
For one more evident token of His goodness and love.

*Ian Caughey*

# CHILDHOOD YEARS

Softly flow those childhood years,
Of happy hearts and blissful tears,
Gentle blossoms on their way,
They break my heart, they can but stay,

Gently falls the springtime rain,
On tender buds that burst again,
That are once more pressed, twixt the pages,
Of childhood years, and cherished ages,

A dimpled smile, a tuneful song,
A moment captured, not for long,
A photograph, those memories,
Of bygone days, and those 'used to be's',

Yes I helplessly behold,
Another story being told,
I embrace my children, both with tears,
Hold close to me, those fleeting years,

Then comforted they fly away,
Like butterflies into the day,
With wings that only take them where,
There's many a year, of strife and care,

It seems we give birth, just to sigh,
For those childhood years, keep fleeting by,
Spring, brings forth another day,
And autumn is not far away.

*C Langdon*

## THANK YOU FOR THE MUSIC
*(To Johnnie Walker, DJ and radio/TV presenter)*

You've known fame and fortune
As a radio star.
In spirit I've been with you
As you've travelled fast and far.
A hippie on a Harley,
Wind blowing through your hair,
Always following your dreams,
Your spirit free as air.

For thirty years I've known you,
How can that be true?
When we are together
You're only twenty-two.
As you recall the memories
Of things that have been
Your voice makes the years disappear
Again I'm seventeen.

Through the radio, I've been there,
With you on the North Sea,
Walked down San Franciscan streets
And gone to Glastonbury.
I shared your joy when your son was born
Played 'Pop The Question' each day
And always there has been music
Somewhere along the way

Looking to the future,
Whatever it may bring,
I'll be there, always wishing you
The best of everything.

*Pamela Evans*

## SILVERY FOG

Slowly, silently
Fog rolls . . . in with the tide,
creeping quietly over fields beside:

Silvery fog blankets hills, town,
and trees.
Fog coming in silently as a shroud.

Grey and cold, misty, white clouds,
closing off the sunshine bright
taking away the beautiful light.

Ah! But the fog has a beauty all its own . . .
The coolness of this fog-laced day,
proves to me Autumn's here to stay.

*Carol Cecelia Olson*

## CARBOOT SALES

Look in front look behind
You'll never know what you'll find
Make an offer no bid too small
I want to get rid of it all
I'm a genuine booter don't know the cost
Over the years fortunes I've lost
But what it's worth I don't care
I'm happy just selling my ware
The profit I make never goes to me
It's all for charity what you see.

*Dawn Moore*

## GUEST OF HONOUR

School in the morning, quarter to nine,
duffel coat fastened, standing in line.
Infants, Juniors, Secondary School,
Pythagoras theory, Fleming's left hand rule.

First job tomorrow, learning a trade,
hard up till Thursday, till I get paid.
Keep to my mother, half what I earn,
rest in my pocket, money to burn.

Friday at last, night on the town,
Benson and Hedges, Newcastle Brown.
Lass on the dance floor gives me the eye,
swagger on over straighten my tie.

Saturday promise, give her some chat,
drinks at the Rovers, back to her flat.
Twittering bed springs, flimsy divan,
cigarette afterwards, now I'm a man.

Woodchip wallpaper, Arabian Glow,
all too familiar, can't wait to go.
Across town like a Tom cat, cold empty street,
home before daylight, sopping wet feet.

Girl at a party, promise to ring,
go out together, married by spring.
Children come later, Adam and Ben,
seems only yesterday, now they're young men.

Retired on Friday, pension and clock,
round the world cruise, time to take stock.
Stroll in country, nice Sunday roast,
family at Christmas, ones I love most.

Big day tomorrow, ride in a hearse,
draughty old chapel, wife reads a verse.
Favourite hymn, loved ones in tears,
I'm guest of honour after seventy five years.

*Nigel W Briggs*



## THE OTHER WOMAN

You were annoyed with me that day
When I told you that I felt used.
I think you felt misunderstood
Whilst I just felt confused.

We made it up - and all was well
The future looked so bright
But my future hopes just faded out
After what I saw tonight.

I saw you both - your wife with you
- about that I didn't care
But I did when you just turned away
As if I wasn't there.

Maybe I had convinced myself
I was the 'only one' all along
But it's taken till tonight to know
That I was oh so wrong.

I enjoyed it all - though secretive
So did you  or so I reckoned
But I think I'll tell you here and now
- No way will I be second.

*Jane Roberts*

## JOURNEY OF A SOUL?

Semi-consciously I dream . . .
Of places that I'm sure I've been?
Of places where I've lived before?
Of times of peace and times of war!
Confusing visions flicker fast,
Revealing hints towards my past.
As mixed-up memories emerge,
The happy and the sad converge.
Partners, families, roles I've played,
Lives I've taken, lives I've saved.
The different bodies I have used,
The lands I've roamed and waters cruised.
- But do these images, of times long gone,
Prove that my own soul lives on?
Will it live to occupy another?
A whole new life, a brand new lover?
Is there truth in what I've seen?
Or are they products of my dream?
When the Reaper comes and I see the light,
I'll hope and pray my dreams were right . . .

*Paul Roberts*


## EYES

The eye of a friend is a good mirror,
The eye of a beloved is a real terror,
It holds and pierces with just a glance,
The eyes of Kevin make the whole world dance.

The eyes of my loved one
Are beautiful beyond compare
Into the eyes of my beloved
To look I once did dare.

What did I see, but love shining there,
More beautiful than the brightest star,
Since then, my heart belongs not to me,
It's gone with Kevin far over the sea!

*Mary Frances Mooney*

## ON EMERGENCE FROM HIBERNATION

I ventured out to view the world
I opened my eyes
And the light made me blind
I emerged from the cave
Inch by inch and day by day
I feel I want to return
But I must be brave

My first faltering footsteps I took
My legs were shaky
For the land felt like the sea
I need to find some equilibrium
And silence this beating drum
That pounds inside of me

Then I breathe in pure clear air
And my joy replaces fear
All the beauty that surrounds
I feel I stand on holy ground

I see the flowers and the trees
And life begins to smell so sweet
I blend and begin to merge

*Ian Barton*

## HOLIDAY TIME

Little cat,
Heart is true.
Chin on paw -
Watching you.
What a welcome
On return.
Will not stray
From your side.
Gentle brush
Over fur.
Sleeps nearby.
Rhythmic purr.
Gently touching
With her paw.
'Are you there?'
Just making sure.

**Alwyn Jolley**


## REASONS TO BE CHEERFUL

Of reasons to be cheerful
Many come my way,
A crackling fire in winter,
The flowers that bloom in May,
The golden sun in summer
Shining on the sea,
The sparkle in your eyes
Each time you look at me,
The warbling of a skylark,
A harvest moon above,
But most of all the knowledge
You have given *me* your love!

**Ailsa Keen**

## UNTITLED

It's like living in a bubble
Floating around on air.
Nobody must enter
Nobody must care.

You can't escape the bubble
There's nothing but darkness there.
No light enters this bubble
It really isn't fair.

The world goes on around you
But inside you can't be seen.
Nobody wants to know you
Nobody hears you scream.

I can't see beyond this darkness
Tell me where to find the light
You can't really, can you?
No-one can help my plight.
So there really is only one answer
But you mustn't shed a tear
Just stick a pin in this bubble
And then I'll just disappear.

***Sue Harper***


## UNTITLED

Poets often conceal their poetry
In their closets,
Whereas I
Conceal my closets
In my poetry.

***Matthew S Brierley***

## My True Love

In Scarborough looking at a seaside view,
That was the place I fell in love with you.
In amongst the sea and golden sand,
You looked at me and I took your hand.

We've been going out ever so long,
because our love is ever so strong.
We've been through so much together,
because I want our love to last forever.

I think of you all the time but that's cool,
because my love for you is a bottomless pool.
You're constantly on my mind because I care,
As long as there's a me and you I want you there.

You are the only one on earth for me,
my heart's all yours, you hold the key.
Your kiss sends shivers down my spine
A cuddle makes me glad you're mine.

*Helen Abel*


## Start Again

As life goes on and time goes by
I often sit and wonder why.
All the things in life which now have passed
But now I must change my life at last.
But oh what will the future be?
I must put my past life behind me.
As I go through life all on my own
I never know where I may roam.
But one day I will find my peace of mind
And perhaps a woman by my side.

*R Muscroft*

## A LOVE I HAVE LOVED

The last of the fields are tilled
my plan of life fulfilled.
Can I sit back and rest?
God knows, I've done my best.
It's the autumn of my days
the last of sunshine rays
when all now stands at peace,
the day's toil begun to cease.
In the sky my star appears
I've wished on it for years
'What omen do you bring to me
to one who is so unworthy?'
'Your journey takes a different way
now, in the evening of your day.
Your many days of sorrow
will end upon the morrow,
your fields full crops will yield
and life you will rebuild.
The sun will shine much brighter
your load become much lighter.'
'Dare I ask how this will be,
what are the changes I will see?'
'Loneliness and sorrow will now end
for here from heaven you have a friend,
He's chosen you, and it's His intent
our favourite angel will be sent.
From the brightest of the stars she came
Hazel . . . that will be her name.'

*Francis Patrick Brown*

## THE SPRING

'In the spring,'
that's what you said.
The words keep turning
in my head.

In the spring
you would be free;
only then
return to me.

Hardened ground
and hardened heart,
all the time
whilst we're apart.

Deep, as earth
protects its seeds,
so I shelter
human needs.

Waiting seems
eternity,
'til the warmth
returns to me

In the spring.
Still here - somehow.
Will you truly
come back, now . . . ?

**Celia Harper**

## STRANGE COMPANION

Boris spun his web,
Across the window space.
It was the home of Margaret,
Who lived in Hansom Place.

He was her strange companion,
For a year or two,
And gave her lots of interest
When she had the summer flu.

The window cleaner could not shift him.
No matter how he tried.
But after a long cold winter,
Sadly, Boris died.

It wasn't the wind and cold
That popped him off real quick.
But a keen eyed blackbird,
Who grabbed him for her chick.

We should not have called 'him' Boris.
For she left a silken sack.
Hiding in the corner,
Of the window's crack.

Then on a warm spring morning
Hanging by silken skein,
Were lots of little spiders.
'Boris' was born again!

**Sandra Simpson**

## A Soldier's Fate

The young soldier was only nineteen,
He hadn't been long in the war.
The horrors the others had seen,
He had not yet saw.

He showed off a bit, with his gun.
Larking around with a mate.
He only wanted a bit of fun,
He'd no idea of his fate.

The fighting started later that day.
The young soldier fought his last fight.
When the bullets came, he was just in the way,
He never made it till night.

Later that night they crept into the wood,
The bodies of friends to recover.
They were lay deep in the mud.
The one who found him - his brother.

They felt for that man,
As he loaded his gun.
Like only a soldier can.
As deep in the woods he ran.

As the bullets tore through the night,
They prayed for his safe return.
It was now his own personal fight.
Another lesson of life to learn.

He was missing for days,
But returned safe and sound.
So my father says.
Not a question was asked,
About being out of bounds,
'Cause they knew he'd completed his task.

His life now wouldn't be the same.
God's will had now been done.
His anger he could never tame,
Another father had lost a son.

*Hilary Ann Torrens*

## GARDENING 1990-92

I made a garden out of a wilderness, I dug and dug the soil
Now as I watch the flowers bloom repaid is all my toil
I hear the birds at dawning, and the cuckoo's call is strong
God's wondrous gift of nature is mine the whole day long
To me the soil is wonderful, He in whom I put my trust
Once also held it in His hands, for man is deity mingled with dust
If I am very silent I may hear the bluebells ring
A gorgeous golden butterfly has just now taken wing
I cannot make one blade of grass, not even a single weed
Oh mighty everlasting God, praise and worship be all my creed
And as I behold my garden, I find humbleness is mine
For in everything that grows there I see the hand of the Divine
I'll never be Keats or Wordsworth, for they were very great
But working in my garden my faith is in full spate
Ofttimes it's like a river that has very turgid grown
Then with aching limbs and blistered hands I realise I'm not my own
On Calvary's cross a price was paid mankind can never know
Lord, as I clear and dig and plant may my devotion grow
In tree and flower and humble weed God's majesty is shown
And we and all creation belong to Him alone.
He made us and He cares for us, whate'er this world may say
If we follow His commandments our obedience He'll repay.

*Amber Gillmeister*

## BEAUTY IN POETRY

I stood transfixed and gazed, with wonder in mine eyes,
At that beauty there before me, my eyes did tell no lies,
My heart was pounding in my breast, my eyes were filled with awe,
When I saw that splendid creature, I could not find a flaw.

The hair upon that lovely head, like a field of ripened corn,
Rippling softly in the breeze, on that sultry warm morn,
Her eyes were so like diamonds, hard chips of molten fire,
This raised a lump within my breast, overflowing with desire.

Those lips so red and rosy, adorned her pretty face,
With the voice of a prima diva, let out with stately grace,
She had the aura of an angel, and a body that belied,
That this lady here before me, was Venus in disguise.

God made this splendid creature, then threw away the mould,
He placed her here upon this land, to be coveted like gold,
This beautiful living creature, that stole away my heart,
My lovely gorgeous angel, from whom I hate to be apart.

**Sandy Laird**


## SUMMER

When the summer comes once more
And one has to carry out a chore
Do not moan and groan
There are other people prone
To the differences in the weather
Near and far even in the heather
Whether in Scotland or London
Spare a smile for one and all, even Spondon.

**A Usher**

## JEREMY

You were still inside my mind
        when I woke this morning
I couldn't shake you out
        or dismiss that look in your eyes
I cleaned the windows
        but your reflection took away my concentration
So I went for a walk
        only to end up at your gate
I had this continual ache inside all through the day
        no Disprin would dissolve it away
For at the bottom of the glass
        your name was written in the remains of the tablet.

*Sarah Barnes*


## UNTITLED

Child of the thirties, born into depression,
Where talents and aspirations, had no chance of expression.
To try and surmount it, you don't stand a chance,
No-one to guide you, in life's great big dance.

No careers officers, so stay in your class,
Find your own way - like walking on glass!
What is my class? Well, I suppose it is working,
So get to it girl, and no bloody shirking!

If only someone would tell me, I could stay on at school,
but do as Mum says - and don't act the fool!

First the depression, then Hitler's aggression,
of this crazy world, I had a wonderful impression!
But through it all, like others I sailed,
The 'Working Class Humour' well,
                it never failed!

*M Knights*

## THOUGHTS OF SPRINGTIME

In the very depths of winter
When the weather is wet and much colder
When days are short and nights are long
And we feel just a little bit older
We suffer colds and flu and sneezes
Sore throats, chesty coughs and wheezes,
Stiff joints, all sorts of aches and pains
The arthritis seems to be worse when it rains,
Out come the long Johns and thermal vests
Thick woolly jumpers to warm the chests
Now the Christmas rush is over
The excitement has died down
Thoughts turn to warmer sunny days
Of lush green fields and bright blue skies
And the golden summer sun
But still it's bleak and miserable
With springtime not quite here
No sign of springtime flowers yet
In our gardens to bring us cheer
The fields and trees all look so bare
No sound of birds singing anywhere
But just a little while longer
Then nature will gloriously yield
There'll be new buds on the trees
And new-born lambs in the fields
Birds will merrily greet each new dawn
The miracle of new life will again begin
God's creation will be in full bloom
Oh! Springtime for me
Cannot come too soon.

**Sue Strachan**

## OLD PENDLE

Old Pendle, Old Pendle, you look down on this land,
And you are ever so grand.

A long time ago the witches flew by,
As they rode across the black sky.

They wore long coats, and big pointed hats,
And they always seemed to have some cats.

Broomsticks they did appear well into the night,
Giving everyone a terrible fright.

Casting spells is what they'd utter,
People were afraid of what they would mutter.

A curse they put on people they did not like
So they tried to avoid them with all their might.

In 1612 in Lancaster they went to their doom,
And not a moment was it too soon.

Now peace reigns over Pendle at long last,
For all of this was all in the past.

Pendle looks lovely when it is full of snow
I was born and bred here so I should know.

From miles around it can be seen
And I hope that you have been

A walk to the top and you will see,
What a wonderful place Pendle Hill can be.

*Valerie E Brown*

## SOLDIER'S WIFE

Together hand in hand
Across many a land
Soldier blue
I have followed you

The man the body the brain
I have watched you train
In sun rain sleet snow or fog
You had to work-out and jog

Morning noon and night
Sometimes we used to fight
An ugly scene
Most of which we did not mean

Caught up in the army net
Hard work and plenty sweat
A man with a mission
I sometimes wondered my position

You signed for ten years
Some of which had plenty tears
Your patience was often tried
I wish I had never cried

My secret I would have to tell
I hope you will take it well
A last we will be a family
Will you accept twins calmly?

**Helen Nelson**

## NATURE'S GRACE

tender in its footsteps, with joy in its arrive.
time has come to love and teach a family to survive.
twigs and grass are woven, no time for a rest
lined with fur and feathers, nothing but the best
eggs sat on patiently, with lots of love and care
and music rings in little chirps, and there is no
time to spare.
wide open beaks, fed equally day by day
flying feathers do appear, then it's all food
and play.
then the nest is left, it has served purpose and
place.
and whistles fill the air, with thanks for
nature's grace.

*Tyron Allbright*

## WASTE OF SPACE

What a waste
This shop so big
What a waste the empty space
With people living
On the streets
What a waste of space
We will squat it
Make it a home
With free cafe
And free food for all
When they come to
Get us out we will
Go in another one
What a waste of space.

*Bob Lewis*

## SOME DAY

Some day you will find,
That quiet attitude of mind.
Which you have often heard about,
But have been far too busy to seek out.
You are now retired - not ruled by clock hands.
So those interests of yours you can expand.
Things you always thought would be fun,
Can now be given a trial run.
At times you wonder how you were able to earn a living.
But you picked up much just through giving,
However it's not until you really survey the past,
That you know how much you've learned that will last.
You've probably dreaded this very day,
But are pleased you have been spared to find a way.
To blaze a trail for younger generations,
Who will most likely experience the same reactions.

*Betty Green*

## DOES GOD CARE?

Does God care when my heart is pained
Too deeply for mirth and song
As the burdens press and the cares distress
And the way grows weary and long.

Does God care when my heart is dark
With a nameless dread and fear as the
daylight fades into deep nightshade.

Does he care enough to be near
Does God care when I've tried and failed
To resist some temptation strong
When in my deep grief I can find no
relief
Though my tears flow all night long.

*J C Leadbeater*


## MY LIFE IS NOW SOLD

I'll make my friend with a spaceman
And run away to the moon
The spirit inside me yearns for change,
To break free from the life-long classroom.

The end of the day stays away
Night-time's the cue to exit,
I've redeemed myself never to fail
Even though everyone expects it.

The ruined earth beneath my feet
Crumbles unwillingly with its defeat,
Fate's telling me to listen to the sun
To run away from childhood
Forgetting everything I've done.

To know and to see my limited appeal,
To hunt, to seek and allow me to feel,
I can't stand alone anymore
I can't break out this mould
The value of my life is now sold.

*Paul Warren*

## THE GIVEN LIFE

I'll scorn not this given life,
Nor will I search my soul for life anew.
I may doubt what lies beyond,
For that I cannot view.

I see the bustle and the pace,
And what I see is just a race.
A race for time that need not be,
For time can only be the past,
And so the moment is for me.

Now I will rise and go, to make my way,
Yes, I will reap my corn.
But most of all whene'er I can,
I'll absorb the day.

*Ken Lowe*


## LEAVE ME BE

The winds of disaffection eased me from my tree,
I became excited, exhilarated, blowing wild and free.
The wind tossed and swirled me everywhere,
Showing feelings and sights, to me, so rare.
But erstwhile, without the sustenance of care,
Devoid of culture, nourishment and fare,
My nature changed and I withered slowly,
I became fragile, forlorn and lowly.
I still enjoyed the freedom of the breeze,
But now I wonder what happened to the other leaves.

*G E Khandelwal*

## NEARLY THERE

Neil Kinnock beat the drum of hope,
He said 'Wake up from your slumbers,'
The late John Smith, with honest fervour spoke,
And said 'You must unite in your numbers.'

These men of vision had the sight,
They knew what must be done,
To write the script, and get it right,
And free the people from their plight.

To rid this land from greed and sleaze,
That's brought the country to its knees,
To right the wrongs, and see fair play,
And let the people have their say.

So Tony Blair has now decreed,
That the people of this country need,
To know that someone really cares
And feel again this land is theirs.

*J Knott*




## I LOVE YOU, JESUS

I love you Jesus,
I love you Lord
as the angels do with one
accord.
Glory and power is yours,
as the Spirit outpours,
His blessings from the
heavenly throne.
With you Jesus.
I feel really at home.

*Paul Gainsford Bailey*

## TRUE HAPPINESS

Each of us that ever lived
Has shared a common quest;
To find true happiness in life,
And be our very best.

But in our daily living
There's a problem that we meet.
It's a silent, nagging feeling;
Something's missing, incomplete.

And in our need to fill this gap
Which feels so deep and wide,
We search for our fulfilment
In the world we see outside.

We try to make more money
And we fill our lives with 'toys',
In the hope that these possessions
Will be transformed into joys.

'If only I had something else,
For then I would be glad.'
Yet deep inside our thirst for more,
We know, would be as bad.

So wherein does the answer lie,
If not the world outside;
For its path to promised happiness
Just failed us when we tried?

The truth was with us all along
But we've been too blind to see;
We need to look within ourselves
If we want to be truly free.

There is a Universe within us
Which, having been unfurled,
Shows us happiness is just a thought
In the way we view our world.

We cannot change the world outside
But if we change the one within,
Transformed by thoughts of harmony,
A new life can begin.

Our thoughts in life are everything
And no-one can take them away.
Whatever you think, so shall you be,
So think great thoughts this day.

*Ian Davison*


## THE BLUE SILK DRESS

He touched her gently, the blue silk quivering under his touch,
His hand moved, wanting her so very much.
Her eyes darkened, her mouth opened, sighing;
She wanted him too, no more crying.
The silk fell to the floor,
He opened the bedroom door.
They dropped to the ground, moaning with passion,
Moving together, completely in love.
Afterwards his hand stroked her cheek,
She looked back at him, so gentle and so meek.
She smoothed his hair and smiled at him,
You could smell their love, the light was dim.
She giggled a pretty little laugh,
And he, loving her, laughed back.
They rose hand in hand, two roses in full bloom,
Kissing they dressed, left the room,
Entered back into the world, doom and gloom.
Until; she smiled again and he smiled too.

*Kellyanne Robertson*

## OH CONCRETE ONE

Building so high,
Concrete never lies.
Blocks out all
The light, drains
my will to fight.
Can't hear myself
breathe, every
colour and creed.
Building so grey,
Like my urban day.
Haunted and eclipsing,
Silently bewitching.
Building so high,
Like gods in the sky.
Oh, concrete one.

Silent Warriors
with double
glazed eyes,
Watching us scuttle
and the lies
that we hide.
Skyline of aerials
Mohican punk giants,
Cast their shadow
in total defiance.

The
green
loses ground
each day to
the grey, as
technology moves
in mysterious ways.
Nature is obsolete
so worship
new News, God
is in colour
with a 13 amp fuse.

**Gary Parker**

## FREE AS A BIRD

I sometimes wish I was a bird, and take off in the sky.
I'd go just where I wanted and fly so very high.
And when my wings began to tire, I'll find a leafy tree.
Tuck my head into my wings and sleep would come to me.
Then when the dawn begins to break, I'd wake and look for food.
Maybe take a bath and find a drink and then I'd feel real good.
I'd have a sense of freedom up there among the clouds.
No worries to deter me an away from all the crowds.
Then if I got too lonely, I'd find myself a mate.
We'd build a nest together and leave the rest to fate.
Then when the winter comes and maybe lots of rain
We'd take off in the sky again and maybe land in Spain.
There, we could be so happy, enjoying all the sun
Just have to keep our eye out for a farmer's gun.
So if I lived my life again, although it sounds absurd.
I think I just would have to be, a happy carefree bird.
Just a feeling to be free, is just the life for me.

*P D Dugdale*


## A TRIBUTE TO MUM

To a mother kind and true
All the gifts I send to you
This special day I send my love
And heartfelt thanks to God up above
Thanks a lot for all the chores
Cooking, washing, ironing,
And cleaning out drawers
Your job seems never done
So spend this Mother's day
Having some fun.

*Margery Blake*

## VESTIGIAL DRUMS

In the oceans of human hypocrisy
Are islands of integrity
To which we cling in hope eternal
That jungle greed of self survival
Will not blind the modern mind:
That civilised men no longer need
The bloody destruction that follows greed.

The rising growth of world production
And intelligent birth control reduction
Insurrection may abate
And poverty eliminate,
But while injustice and iniquity
Contaminate society
Vestigial jungle drums are beaten
'Eat them or *we'll* be eaten'.
And from this crime and violence flows
Inevitably as winter snows.

Preserve my privileged status quo,
The sleazy crook will loudly crow.
What care I for grief and sorrow
I bequeath to child tomorrow?

If in experiment Earth
Babe is memory void at birth
And only begins to learn at three
The universal mystery:
To procreate, but before oblivion
Perchance the hyper-sensitive 'soft-ware' brain
May sometimes glimpse a higher plane
Of mystic and enchanted isle
That to his suffering brings a smile

Of hope that he - student universe-ity -
Will learn by experience of earthly pain
And quality to live again
To reach the ultimate perfection
On The-Day-Of-Resurrection.

*Theodore L Alder*

## NIGHTMARES

Be still, be quiet my child
The demons do not exist
Only in your head they kill
Shut them out, don't let them in.

Be still, be quiet my child
Morning will soon awake
And sunshine will defeat the dark
All will be peace again.

Be still, be quiet my child
For God is loving you, holding you
In his gentle warm hands of his
Like a baby in its mother's cradle.

Be still, be quiet my child
Think only happy thoughts tonight
Let go of the bad ones, switch the channel
Lie on your other side, then go to sleep.

*Bethany Fowler*

## Humour

i've a funny sense of humour
shouldn't always laugh
when i see a kilt
round a neck like a scarf
when you see the tins fall down
in the supermarket
there's a deadly hush
then people start laughing
sometimes i have to smile
can't laugh out loud
if i'm in a church
or with a posh crowd
at a christmas panto
with tiny tots
saying and doing things
makes me laugh a lot
they say laughing is good for you
of this i am sure
when you're feeling low
it's just like a cure.

**Lottie Bugler**


## Georgia

Georgia, with your soft brown skin,
Your easy smile and sense of fun,
You turn all heads and win
The hearts of everyone.

Your elegant style and confident walk,
Your beauty is for all to see.
People can't help but talk
Now that you are three.

**Helen Cronin**

## MUSIC AT THE CREATION OF LIFE, FADES WITH DEATH

A child is born, his mother feels pain, then joy,
for his cries are music to her ears.

The child grows, his laughter, his tears bring
pleasure, serenading his mother through each passing day.

The boy becomes man, his voice not yet broken,
crystal clear, echoes through the church,
rippling past ears of young and old.

Man becomes maestro, upon a stage.
Tapping his baton lightly on a metal stand.
The music unfolds like a mighty roar
as an army into battle.

Imaginary notes, crotchets, quavers
dance amongst the musicians, tormenting
all with their heads and tails.
Time passes, the man is old, his spirit leaves his body.

He sees a box, long and black, draped neatly
with a cross of flowers, sliding into the unknown.
The music that accompanied the creation of his life,
now accompanies him to death with voices sad and low.
It is here, the symphony ends.

*Jennifer Polledri*

## THE DANCER

He danced for life:
First a slow waltz and then a quickstep.
Each stage of development introducing a new rhythm
Each rhythm creating a new dance.

He danced for love:
Leaping and prancing; an acrobat,
Vital and skilful; beautiful body and sensitive mind.
Drunk on the sweet wine of womanhood.

He danced the seasons:
The fertile, ripe seeds of his future
Planted carefully in his past - his reward a fine harvest.
Firm fruits of friendship, eternal love.

He danced for wars:
Discordant conflict and confusion.
Feet stamping and body jerking to the rhythmic percussion.
Heart bursting with patriotic pride.

He danced for death:
Alone;
In silence;
Without moving.

*P A Minson*


## MOTHER'S RUIN

No bayonet or bullet could have pierced my heart like this
And no marksman could have hit the spot more surely
You cut me down unmercifully, relishing the sight
Now parade your peacock feathers, dance upon me

The sometimes lucid intervals seem all too far away
And the effort to remember not worthwhile
But still I find I'm haunted by the gentle kick inside
And cannot submit my love to that denial

***Kim Montia***


## TRASH WITH CASH

I've always bin one to be out 'avin' fun
An' when I was a nipper at school
I thought it was great to keep turnin' up late;
Bein' stupid 'n' actin' the fool.

They said 'You'll get nowhere with that attitude!'
But I told 'em, 'I couldn't care less!'
An' I ain't done bad; bin a bit of a lad
Though there's bin some 'ard times I confess.

Me mate got a job an' it pays a few bob
Though as 'e says, 'It's never enough.'
But work ain't for me; I just like to be free,
I was never cut out for that stuff.

Now I'm on a cruise 'n' it's all fags 'n' booze
An' I'm 'avin' the time o' me life.
Got me eye on a bird, so don't say a word
If you 'appen to meet with the wife!

I've made it at last! What a change from the past.
Drinkin' life from a solid gold cup.
It's strange but it's true; I've done better than you
'Cos me lottery number's come up!

***Dennis Turner***

## TO DYLAN THOMAS
*(or the ball that never touched the ground)*

The bright-eyed boy of passion came running down the street
A curly-headed angel with firefly in his feet.

On autumn days he'd linger through the misty mildewed glass
And hear the scream of the white-faced gull and the sea-soaked rain clouds pass
Though his father named him after the Prince of all that's dark
He would never know the burden of that Mabinogion mark.

The run-down rickety Fernhill where he spent a happy hour
Fed his imagination like a honey bee feeds a flower
A muddy hay-strewn Eden was to fill his later life
In the stark and sorry city, like an artist's palette knife.

By education's hard stone wall he kept the round and burning ball
Of sunlight; inside his rough note pad
And only in his father's room
Exposed the precious gift he had.

At Laugharne and the bobbing sea
Where the salt-fish hit the bobbing quay
And the muddy walk to a half-mast boat
Where the birds can't fly and the storm clouds gloat,
This strange and lonely cockle-shell town
A wind-storm away from settling down.

The American Dream held him hard in its stead
But defying defeat could not put him to bed
Once more to the platform he dragged himself on;
Once more to the mercy of student and don.

In the black depths of coma, though his brain lay asleep
His heart cried out 'Laugharne'! though his spirit lay deep.
To Under Milk Wood, to the love of his past
He could lay in her arms; he was peaceful at last.

'O sweet-tongued man of passion-so shall your voice be free'!
'Time held you green and dying though you sang in your chains like the sea'.

*Barbara King*


## THE PIANISTS

She sat beneath the apple tree, her hands
Clasped loosely, uselessly, on rug-wrapped knees
While through an open window rippled scales
Played on a piano with practised ease.
In silent echo clumsy fingers stirred
Recalling skills learnt in her teenage days . . .
A pause, some random chords, and then she heard
The first few bars of Chopin's Polonaise.

She smiled, remembering the piano roll
Which made her mother think she practised still
While she, tired of it, read a library book.
A girl sat laughing on the window sill -
'Granny, don't tell, it's you who's playing now;
The tape you gave me at Christmas last year.
If mum finds out there'll be a dreadful row.'
'I did the same. Both skills and sins we share.'

They smiled again, two minds thinking as one,
Content with music and the April sun.

*Gwen Joselin*

## MRS T

There was a lady in our village, who has just passed away.
A very lovely lady you hear the people say.
She had a word for everyone, she met upon the street.
Hello! How are you today? Would the little one like a sweet -
Peeping in a new baby's pram standing outside the shop -
Then home to knitting pins. To knit a baby top.
Next day she would call round, with coat and hat for baby
A chat and a cup of tea, she was a lovely lady.

Mrs Taylor lived in a little village called Austrey.
But the villagers named her Mrs T.
Her plum coloured coat covered her jolly frame.
Smile upon her face, Austrey won't be the same.
She was a wife and a mother, a friend to all she knew.
People she did not know, well, that was just a few.
You might say who am I? How do I know?
Mrs T was my mum and I loved her so.

*Linda Taylor*


## THE WEB OF LIFE

The spider spins her web
like an old woman at her loom.
Waiting for her task to end,
for her pleasure is their doom.
They don't see the danger in her silken thread,
Nor do they fear its soft embrace
this ethereal shroud,
That cloaks them with life's snares.
Unseen by mortal souls
Creatures of their petty worlds
She'll catch them unawares.

*Lana J Povey*

## OUR FUTURE PEACE

Above the blue and sacred earth,
The sun from heaven shines its rays,
Not missing in its path a mark,
That passes down through space and lays.

My fear of an eternal hell,
Through nuclear holocaust to dome,
And people here who live in peace,
Of soul and mind of every home.

Who is a man to say to his fellow,
Human race if forced to fight,
In days of peace and blessed night,
Only provocation will cause the fear when all is right.

I pass my days in wondering,
When I will have my share,
Of love and understanding,
Which is for all I care.

The work for man is never left to fall into decay,
For food and drink and entertainment,
Are called for every day,
So let them have their way.

In peace I pray that I might be,
That brings forth work in pleasure,
More enjoyable than making war,
That we all have the best of leisure.

Patience is the only thing,
Which we are left to culture,
God's grace and peace are ours to keep,
In this world for our future.

*Michael Westlake*

## THE REASON

His love outstanding to his early grave - and
far beyond - Christ's outstanding love - for all man -
kind - was the reason - that he came to earth - and -
died - love he showed for his Father's works - when
he gave up life on earth - dear God - you now have
him close by you - his new position - on his return to -
Above - is to rule as King - and act as judge - when your -
days of days arrive on earth - arrive to bring an end -
to all the wicked ways of man - that dwell around -
the globe - a day when - the earth will be set free -
from endless pains - and the pangs of death itself returns -
to a paradise park - no wars on earth - taking place -
no one dying of hunger - while others - throw food -
away - each one living - will have a place to dwell - a
place of peace - what are we talking about - God's kingdom
on this very earth - come Lord Jesus - come quickly

Amen and Amen

*R P Scannell*

## TAKING OUR FOOD FOR GRANTED!

People around this world
Hardly getting through a year,
Hunger and starvation.
It makes me shed a tear.

It's horrible what you hear on the news.
Each and every day,
Seeing innocent people
Their bodies just flaking away.

They do not deserve
What they are going through,
Diseases at all angels
Unlike me and you!

*Laura Keightley (14)*


## QUESTIONS, QUESTIONS, ALWAYS QUESTIONS

He's only after knowledge when ignorance rules
and the sage is the exception and the masses are all fools
to be swayed by any Philistine who leads them by the nose
with promises of who knows what that melt away like snows.

He ponders on the meaning of the universe and life
when the television pictures show a world that's torn with strife
to a background hymn about a God of love and peace and good
and the camera turns towards the babe clothed only in its blood.

He's in search of solace for a restless, searching mind
yet wants the kind of still and peace that only the dead can find
when having run life's course and sickened at the rising pace
are pleased to settle their account and quit the mortal's race.

He dwells upon the glorious past, the golden age that's been;
and tales that tell of times now gone which cast a happier scene
despite the disease and famine, the oppression, the workers' sadness
and not forgetting slavery, child labour, oh! and genocidal madness.

He's only after answers when questions abound
and the questions keep on coming but there's no-one around
to give an honest verdict on the problems on his mind
leaving him to conjure with answers that the politicians find.

*J A Gray*

## THE ODD JOB MAN

Ron is a slowly plodding man
Who moves on heavy feet.
He owns a pipe exuding smoke
As he walks along the street.

Shoulders hunched, and head bent low
He makes a bulky sight.
As he potters round the garden
He works with all his might

You never see him idling
He can always find a task
He eats his sandwich from a tin
And drinks coffee from a flask

He cuts the hedge along our wall
And works with pride and skill.
He then comes over to our side
And tidies with a will.

He does the shopping for the old
And odd jobs for the frail
Gets their pensions once a week
And often posts the mail

So let us spare a kindly thought
For people such as he
He makes the world a nicer place
And helps the old stay free.

*F J Groves*

## HARROGATE

People think Harrogate as a wealthy place,
Maybe in days gone by, in many a case,
Stray's the first eye catcher, unable to build on,
This should stand forever, protested King John,
There are healing waters and springs called the Spas,
The landed gentry, come from so near and far,
The Conference Centre, built twenty years ago,
Should have brought visitors, little did they know,
It promised so much, attracting many shows,
On this front it failed, big names but they don't go,
And seats were expensive, costing twenty pounds,
Even the rich refused, they stood their ground,
Harlow Car Gardens with its high entrance fees,
With all those alpines, roses, and all kinds of trees,
The hybrid species, they need plenty of peat,
Once know as a haven, a rich folks' retreat,
The Valley Gardens, with child's paddling pool,
You can't get near it when the kids are off school,
The Cricket Ground, it is kept with such splendour,
Professionals and youths sharing the agenda,
Also golf, rugby and badminton, to name a few,
Gymnasiums aplenty, stand in a queue,
In the spring there is a renowned flower show,
One year it collapsed, with the weight of the snow,
To the south, east and west are the Yorkshire Dales,
Go north and you see York, known as the Vales
The Minster and Shambles, to name but a few,
All tourist's attractions are well worth the view.

***Ann Dulon***

## INTERPRETING

No-one seems to listen
In this age of rush and speed
We dash ahead, do not care
To life we pay no heed

It's only when we are feeble
Do we stop awhile and ponder
If we just be still and contemplate
We soon begin to wonder

At the incredible law and order
That exists in human form
The systems working in unison
That is the law - that is the norm

When the system's out of harmony
The body plainly tells us
If we listen and interpret
To action it impels us.

For the pounding heart is saying
The body's out of balance
By rushing, fear and fretting
Wasting energy and talents

An expectant mother's fancying
Is the body's way of saying
It needs these vital nutrients
For the babe that it is feeding

When we've pain and we suppress it
Before we've learnt its lesson
We'll make the same mistake again
There's no healing just transgression

So let's listen to the body
Which tells us all we need
To put things right when they go wrong
Efficiency indeed.

*D I Bryden*

## PEACE OF MIND

In the corner of my eye I see a dove;
He is singing for salvation and for love.
Through my eyes this dove is velvet
And his wings are made of gold
And he is flying to find heaven, up above.

In the corner of my eye I see the rain
It is falling for depression and for pain
Through my eyes this rain is acid
And it burns my very soul
I did once hope I would not feel this way again.

In the corner of my eye I see the stars;
I see the planets such as Jupiter and Mars
Through my eyes the sky's a blanket
And the stars are precious jewels,
This lovely picture drowns out buildings, noise and cars.

In the corner of my eye I see our land
I see the consequences of our each demand;
Through my eyes this endless suffering
Is not what we should see;
How can we be so selfish? I don't understand.

*Lisa Corcoran*

## THE WALK

When I'm feeling down and blue
I have a thing I like to do
To walk beside the craggy rocks,
No bills, or worries or ticking clocks.
Along the shoreline I go to muse
When I'm feeling down and blue.

The screaming gulls for company,
Fears and doubts, I have so many.
If I listen to the waves,
'Cheer up' they say, 'now behave'.
You have so very many blessings,
And the worries you are addressing
are like ripples in the sea,
just grains of sand like you and me.
When your problems overwhelm you,
Think of all those others who,
have no home, no family,
Be in good cheer, not down and blue.

And so as the waves sweep in and out,
I hear the children laugh and shout
and watch my husband, kind and good
and start to feel the way I should.
Be grateful for what you have, it's true,
It's no good feeling down and blue.

***Cheryl Mann***

## A Candle Burns

Somewhere in heaven a candle is burning,
Somewhere on earth, hearts are yearning,
Somewhere in heaven, an angel sings,
A new member has joined, and collected their wings.

Sat on a cloud of silver lining,
Whilst people down below, on earth, are pining,
Heaven opened its gates,
You entered the world of angels and saints.

You closed your eyes, had a rest,
And God as you know, takes the very best,
At your feet a flock of doves,
Peace to all the ones he loves.

And as they rejoice up in the sky,
Broken hearts on earth still cry.

*K Baiton*


## A Sobering Thought

Thoughts of war begin to die,
As I see your twinkling eye,
So innocent, so true, so pure,
I hope you never see a war;
So many soldiers lose their lives,
Leaving children and their wives,
Thank the Lord for your father's return,
Take heed, for it's a lesson learned;
Fighting for your country's sake,
Can sometimes be a costly mistake,
As you grow and learn the rules,
Remember that fighting is just for fools.

*N E Evans*

## THE WIND

The wind dominates the gentle calm of space
crushing the sensitive, murdering the Grace;
rattling and scattering the swooning faint-hearted
misleading the sleepy, testing life, tormenting,
from ease departed;
it fights and froths in howling delight
raising and falling with all its might.
Assails the wind, penetrating protections,
displaying its war dance in challenging rejections,
beckoning in wails, its opposition trapping
and demanding; recognition to steal.
Teasing forthrightly, a world to possess.
Never, when held,
its secret to confess.

*Marion Elvera*



## MY SHEPHERD

To walk along those
Fields so green.
Fills my heart with peace serene.
For even here amongst his sheep.
I see love, while lambs do sleep.
Then those cattle they run on by.
Drawn to high ground,
When danger is nigh.
It's then I know, I am
From his other flock.
With the Good Shepherd
Watching upon solid rock.

*R Wright*

## REMEMBER ME

Today, I walked down memory lane,
And to the eye, all seemed the same,
But, love is lost, of long ago,
I remembered, how I loved you, so.
The place just looked the same, as when . . .
I left you alone, back there and then,
At that time . . . it seemed the thing to do.
But how I regret, the hurt I caused you.
Now, looking back, and thinking it through,
I never should have walked out on you.
But at that moment, it seemed so right,
I wanted love . . . I didn't want to fight,
Maybe, if we'd have talked it through,
I would still be there with you.
You and the children, I am missing,
While I sit here . . . reminiscing,
If I could only turn back time . . .
I wouldn't be writing you this rhyme,
Our hearts would still be so entwined,
Oh . . . how could I have been so blind?
But I've lost you now, forever more,
Of this one thing . . . I can be sure.
And you will never see my tears . . .
That I have prolonged, throughout the years,
And you will never, ever know . . .
How I regret, letting you go.
My love for you, will linger on,
Until my dying breath has gone.
Remember me, darling, this I pray . .
Remember me . . . on our wedding day.

*Deana Houghton*

## WISE GAMBLING

I am a keen racing fan and many's a day
I went to the racecourse in hopes it would pay,
There were days when I won and some when I lost
But I enjoyed the excitement without thinking of cost.

Some punters around gave tips on each race
But if you should take them you got egg on your face,
I always had faith in the horse I was choosing
And at the end of the day it wasn't much I was losing.

I have visited Ascot, York and Carlisle
And in winning and losing I enjoyed this the while
But there are some cannot stop and gamble it all
Then their family are left with nowhere-with-all

I think they are wrong and should turn a new leaf
Whereby their families are not left with this grief
Where one hurts the family with gambling addiction
It is time he bet wisely and with a bit of restriction

**Lachlan Taylor**


## AUTUMN MORNING

Morning dew upon the ground
Wets the feet that early tread
And moisture droplets beauty show
The fineness of the spider's web

Mist in veils that ghostlike hang
Without supports in cloaking shrouds
Until the rising sun breaks through
Its rays to reach the waiting ground

No more the dampness on the cheek
That into every crevice creep
But warming sunlight utters forth
To waken nature from its sleep.

*Ian Martin*


## WALKING IN THE RAIN WITH MAN'S BEST FRIEND

Walking in the rain
With man's best friend
Dirty boots and muddy paws
Sloshing through rain sodden forest floors
It could be a nature ramble
But there's no time to smell the flowers
As we speed on through the showers

Walking in the rain
With man's best friend
Both getting soaked to the skin
We must be crazy to begin
It could be a nature ramble
But there's no time to watch the birds
As we speed on like they've not been heard

Walking in the rain
With man's best friend
As the rain runs down our backs
The sky is just as black
It could be a nature ramble
But there's no time to talk to trees
As we speed home for a bath and then tea

*Ian Barton*

## Labour's Victory

Congratulations to you, our Prime Minister Mr Blair.
You campaigned continuously, showed conviction
Stood tall and proud, endured the opposition.
Steadily you raised our spirits, gave us hope,
For this you earned our trust and gained our votes.

It had been many a year, since last I voted
But now, I had enough of all this Conservative gloating.
So off I marched, to my local polling station
Labour got my cross, local and national elections.

May 2nd, brought massive joy and celebrations
A hot and humid day, one I'll always remember.
For Labour had won, the Conservatives went under.
You're in number 10, me next door, on cloud nine.
The votes had mattered, one of them was mine.

**Stephanie Bones**


## The Ladybird

The ladybird has black spots
And he can't tie knots
Underneath his coat of red
Is a small brown furry head

The ladybird so pretty and small
When hibernating curls to a ball
At the end of his feelers are nippers
And he wears small brown furry slippers

**Alison Campbell**

## PRELUDE TO NORMANDY
*(Operation Jubilee, Dieppe August 19 1942)*

    On to that shore
    Danger before
    Dared the brave

    On to that shore
    Danger before
    Sleep the sleep of the grave

    On to that shore
    Danger before
    Freedom was served in your quest

    On to that shore
    Danger before
    None shall disturb your rest

    On to that shore
    Danger before
    Honour is yours

Onward they went forward they went dared the bold
By the powers that deemed surprise it would seem would test
The strength of the tyrant's hold
The price was freedom's life or death the free world had to know
How far advanced in the principles of radar the enemy were and
How strongly entrenched were the foe
At dawn of the chosen day from the mother ships the landing
Craft headed for the enemy shore
Inside the assault craft the Canadians were bonded by duty and
Esprit de Corps
History records history accords the price of freedom was paid
During the hellish hours of that dawn raid
From the assault craft ramps many a man gained the beach
To mortally fall
Honouring with valour England's Commonwealth call
        We shall not forget their sacrifice.

*Sir MacGregor Fletcher*

## ELECTION FEVER MAY 1997

Oh! Mr Major what shall we do?
Shall we vote for Mr Blair
Or shall we vote for you?
There's also Paddy Ashdown and lots of others too
It's all so confusing we really haven't a clue.
Shall we choose Red or Green or maybe Yellow or Blue?

The time has arrived to make a decision
To collect our thoughts with focused precision.
Eeny, meeny miny mo, put on your coat!
Set off to vote! And Go! Go! Go!

Tomorrow there'll be lots of tension
As well as hours of apprehension
Till the hour of ten o'clock draws nigh
When in each part of this great nation
The doors will close at each and every polling station

It's 'Action Stations' throughout the night
As the votes are counted out of sight
Reporters will be busy and the media in a tizzy
News! News! News! All night and day
On radio and TV. You can't get away
From this election fever

Soon after months of conferring and waiting,
Sparring, insulting, promoting, debating,
The final result will be due.
On Friday we'll know without any doubt
Which Party has made it 'right through'
Until then my friends it's all up to you
Whichever you choose 'twill be in the news
The Red or the Green or the Yellow or Blue

***Thelma Barnes***

## SILAS MARNER

The lonely weaver wends his way through dim-lit lane and over field
And happy in his chosen craft, his love of linen is revealed
But life then deals a bitter blow and ignorance plays its own cruel part
The weaver wrongfully outcast, the Church betrayed the purest heart.

As shadows lengthen 'cross his room - the flickering firelight dancing red
The weaver's eyes rest on his loom, his body on his bed
He seeks poor solace in his gold and hoarding as a miser will
His mind grows bitter, his body ill.

Now as his figure picks its way through land and field, his wares to sell
With body hunched and stooping low and eyes so dim they hardly see
His gold has given him no love nor kept him warm through winter night
No comfort has he thus derived from its harsh and brilliant sight.

And then one eve whilst in a trance, he wakens to the cold white gloom
To find a child so fair of face, such innocence abounds his room
He knows his gold has been returned and makes a promise there and then
He'll raise this orphan as his own - his life is to begin again.

The years pass by, his faith restored
He sits and contemplates his past
How rich in love he has become
He makes his peace with God at last.

As slave to the loom, his life was spent
God showed him grace, his soul was content.

***Stephanie Fulfit***

## UNTITLED

Stop what you're doing
And listen up now
The whole world is dying
But I don't know how -
How to stop the world from spinning,
Spinning out of control
Just stop what you're doing
And help us now.

People are dying
Here and everywhere
Your friends, family and neighbours
Need your help
And all of us should share,
In the grief and the sorrow.
But the whole world goes on
As if they don't even care.

The animals the flowers,
The trees and shrubs
Are all going to suffer
If we don't watch out.
Children with asthma, cancer or AIDS
We need to find help before it's too late.
The singing, the laughing where did it all go,
To hell, so the devil can eat up and chew.

What happened to the playgrounds,
The swings and slide,
The children who were laughing
And happy outside?
The hospitals are closing
Because they are full,
Full of those children
That we once knew.

Some die before their parents,
Who are in a state of shock,
As they bury their children
Six foot under in a box.
They wish to swap places,
To give them a chance
To see the world just for a last glance.

But why should they bother
The kids are better off dead,
Safe from the pain and sorrow
This world creates.

*Ann Thomas*


## UNFATHOMABLE RICHES

No eye can see the glory
of the wonders of his Kingdom,
No mind could grasp or fathom
The treasures stored in heaven.

No ear could believe what it heard,
As it sounds too good to be true,
No tongue could speak of all God's goodness,
And what's in store for you!

He has made way for us to enter in,
As by his blood we're cleansed from sin,
There is no fee the entry's free,
He's made a way for you and me.

So get your ticket to Heaven
And you will find it's true,
That poems could not describe how real it is,
And neither can you.!

*Julie McKenzie*

## THE NEW IMAGE

My hair was grey and tied in a bun,
I looked all of a hundred and one,
Deciding I had got in an awful rut,
I made the decision to have my hair cut.

Why not dye your hair too? I thought,
Keep it natural I'd always been taught.
So I thought it would be good to go back,
To the colour I was born with, ebony black.

Sitting in that chair I began to shake,
This was a big step I was about to take.
The hairdresser snipped and she snapped,
Your hair is full of split ends, she rapped.

She applied the colour and left it for a while,
Rinsed it, then cut it into a glamorous style.
Teased it, pulled it, blew it into shape,
Said, 'How's that?' Showed me and removed the cape.

I went home, walking completely on air,
Revelling in the fact, that people did stare,
Many had not seen me with short black hair,
But the impact the style had, I was fully aware.

I have a new image, as you can see,
But really I'm still the same old me.
I have not changed one iota inside,
I'm still five foot tall and two foot wide.

*Patricia Dickson*

## SEEKING

I seemed to *know*
quite long ago
I seemed to grasp the task
I seemed to *know* the Mission
without ever the need to ask!

Just what *was* it then - that happened
as I piled *confusion* - on my path?
Just how was I distracted?
*When* did I forget to laugh?

Why was I full of sorrow
Why did I struggle so
Where had all the joy gone?

*I really didn't know!*

***Sylvia Lee***


## EMBRYO

I had a bad dream, I was naked
In a crowded room, nowhere to hide.
I had a bad dream, all I ever learnt
Turned out to be one big lie.
I had a bad dream, the world was lonely
Full of violence, hate and pain.
I had a bad dream, I was stuck with Elvis
Singing 'My Way' again and again.
I had a bad dream, you said you loved me
And stamped a bar code on my head.
I had a bad dream, I was falling
Didn't cross my heart and now I'm dead.

***Gary Parker***

## MY SON

How can I place pen to paper
And write of the words inside
And tell of my tall son Bobby
How much I have feelings of pride
I remember when young he was crying
At the snow as it lay on the ground
How his small hands were cold and frozen
As he wee sledge went over the mound
I remember each time at the Gala
In our village it came once a year
His mother, dear Mary was laughing
At Bob in his old Highland gear
I remember a brave man of seven
As springtime began in the year
A fair haired young man was crying
By my side
We had both lost somebody dear
I remember a man in his glory
He was wearing his old Highland gear
His sword and his targe he did carry
As he ran through the hills with the deer
His hair and his beard were like the sunset
As it shone on the evening sky
And the feelings I have inside
I will have till the day I die.

*John Redmond*

## POETRY IS

What is poetry - a few written words
Or silent screams gone unheard
Ink on paper - what does it mean
A way of expressing, feelings unseen.
Or does it have meaning between the lines
Of unspoken words - that were undermined
Pushed back by anger, hurt, often shame
A way of releasing the deepest of pain
For what is poetry, if one cannot see
Deep into words as deep as can be
Reading the surface is easy but when
You read with your heart - you'll read it again
And so what is poetry - poetry to me
Expressing my feelings as so to be free
For words are not heard unless they're let out
This is what poetry is all about.

*F Gilpin*


## SILENT MOON

I wept upon the silent moon
you were gone and all was gloom,
till somewhere in the silent night
a bird did call,
such beauty I could scarcely call,
as if the angels from heaven did fall,
but upon the ground,
lay a fallen owl,
whose eyes brightened up the night,
for as it flew into the sky,
I realised,
how free I was just like the bird,
to wing into another world.

*Matthew Longfoot*

# THE JOLLY BOYS' OUTING

Aunty Bet's hair has frizzed
And it's party time tonight
The make-up I have just put on
Makes me look a fright

Put my new blue shoes on
They are feeling rather tight
They're the only ones that match my dress
So they have to be alright

Bill and Bob are grumbling
They just don't want to go
Still they say the really must
Because it's the boss's show

Now at last we are on our way
And pull up at the door
Hear the laughter from within
As we step inside the hall

Soon both are propping up the bar
A glass in hand and not a care
They may have brought us to this do
But they don't know we are there

Oh what hypocrites they are
They are as happy as can be
The only wallflowers seen around
Are Aunty Bet and me

*Adela Llewellyn*

## When Darkness Hits Reality

In my world it's so dark I'm longing to
See the light.
My mind has been affected by this darkness.
I need to be brought into the light.

When will I see the light of day?
The light will help me in every way.
When will I see the light of day?
Please let it be today.

People who live in the light will never
Understand the day when darkness hits
Reality.

It's just another day in the dark for me.
Take me out of the darkness and into
The light.
You know it's right.

People who live in the light will never
Understand the day when darkness hits
Reality.

A day in the dark is a living hell.
Please make me well and bring me into
The light.
Please make the right choice for me
Tonight.

*Paul Hallows*

## THE DANCER

Looking back it is hard to believe,
The young-hearted woman is gone.
It was a secretive race for life,
Now the battle is lost, not won.

We didn't quite click,
At the first meet.
I couldn't stretch that low,
I had two left feet!

The dancer was graceful,
Elegant, reserved.
I was all clumsy,
It was drama I preferred.

But Edna made it fun,
Putting us to the test.
The scissors and the stretch,
The iron cross, she like best.

Her quirky clothes cheered us,
As we put up a fight.
And tried to get noses to the floor,
While instructed to look bright.

The dances, like her,
Were vibrant and quick.
Young and fun loving,
She'd take no stick!

A wonderful woman,
Who would fill me with joy.
As we mastered her moves,
Worked out her ploy.

I'll miss Edna greatly,
Although she said not to cry,
This is my way, not to forget,
But to say goodbye.

*Marie Akers*


## HYMN FOR YOUTH

Look up, look up, O young ones,
Look up to Heaven above,
Don't let this sad world's pleasures
Lure you away from God.
For He is our Creator,
Our lives to Him we owe
And He sent His Son to earth
Because He loved us so.

Speak out, speak out, O young ones,
Speak out for Christ, our Lord.
Don't let the devil tempt you
To question God's own Word.
Tell others of our Saviour
Who died in agony
That we might have a future
With him eternally.

Give praise, give praise, O young ones,
Give praise to God above,
For He has richly blessed us
And shields us with His love.
Remember He has promised
To be with us each day
And He will guide our footsteps
Along life's earthly way.

*Margaret Haining*

## His Own World

call them to come back
come back to planet earth
in the end you
must see the wrongs
of all your ways
andrew sammy was a
dirty rotten vile monster
use a carpenters saw
to bend back his ears
he was a natty girl
playing at being a man
your manliness many said
made him look so glum
like he had drank

lots and lots of beer
till it made him go
off into his own world
sammy andrew sammy led
them all into paths
of sheer utter madness
like he was a god
over all the ancients
weeds and cabbages was
what he had for brains
an illusion that fooled
no souls due their worth
truly you were brainless
who encoded negative values
in your mind and soul

**Richard Clewlow**

## TRUST

Trust is a hard emotion
To contain
Once hurt it is indeed very
Hard to trust again
Friendships do get stronger
Given time they may become
A very special relationship

Although it's very scary
You should give it a try
If that's what you want

It is best to take things slowly
Although emotions don't always allow
I just wish you'd let me in
A bit more

I want to be your friend
A special friend
I want you to tell me
When you're happy or sad
I wouldn't want to hurt you
Or even make you mad
All I want is you to
 . . . trust me

Don't think too much about
The future
What it holds, or brings
Just think about the present
And all those little things
That make you happy

So think about the present
And what you want from life
And talk to me a little more
Don't let trust rule your life

*Kirsten Mason*

## LATCHKEY DAYS

Wearing pieces of string tied round our little necks,
                              each holding a front door key
Was a way of life for several years for my big sister and me.
She'd take me to school each morning, at night she'd be there
                                                    at the gate
Together we walk round the corner, by a laundry we both would wait
A hand would push open a window, a purse with a couple of quid
Would be offered down with two shopping bags, we were the
                                                    latchkey kids.

With errands all done we'd head for home with no-one there to see
Her lighting the fire to warm the house or peeling the spuds for tea.
She'd tidy up as best she could before the others came in
Kettle would bubble upon the stove, ashes thrown into the bin.
Then we'd sit down with a nice hot drink, jam butty to eat and then
She'd lay the table for all of us, not bad for a kid of ten.

Wearing night-dresses made of wincyette, we'd climb the wooden hill
To dream of the time we'd be out of there we could hardly wait until
The day arrived and we'd be free, we'd have our own front door
And to that cold forbidding place we needn't go anymore
The years went by, we both grew up and went our separate ways
To let time heal the void inside created by latchkey days.

***Gillian McGimpsey***

## Untitled

These days we don't rely
upon the horse and cart
to pull a plough along
or to pull a carriage to market
we use a horse powered engine
to take us to and fro
we still rely upon the sheep for wool
and a guide dog for the blind
In the past an oxen
would pull a heavy load in the past
a parrot would be taken down a mine
to fine out where the gas
and save a load of men.
In the past a message
could be sent by a carrier pigeon
In some countries now friendly as they are
an elephant carries passengers
cows still give us milk
unless you like goat's milk,
cats give us companionship
whatever your animal, reptile or
furry type, I hope it's a friend
to you as mine is to me.

*J Dunkley*

## Misty Memories And Clear Tomorrows

As I sit here in my high rise suburban flat,
I wonder what passers-by will think of that.
I sit alone wondering 'why'?
And all this wondering makes me cry.
I sit and remember old hopes and dreams.
Of long summer days and cold ice-creams.

They are old memories, nothing more.
Memories in diaries, upon the floor.
My memories are misty, cloudy with age.
I look at my life, and am filled with courage.
Yet, with each new tomorrow,
My heart fills with sorrow,
Because, although I remember today,
Shall I remember tomorrow or the following day
So it is all misty memories and clear tomorrows.

*Jennifer Flint*


## Foreword

The postman comes in his
Red van, with parcel
To twenty pence letter,

He drops a gas bill through
your door,
To make you feel much better:

But do not despair because
you are not there
Stressed by dire charges -

Shelve that bill,
Which makes you ill
There is a greater largess.

Retire from the ratty race
And read among the pages:
you may a little Kudos gain
The true desire of ages.

*David Hazlett*


## SPECIAL WAY

First of all
There is my
Husband Paul

Al is the one
I know through
Radio alone
Even the telephone

Paul is from Lancs
For which I give
Thanks

Al Dupres is the friend
On the other
End

For I love both
Of them in my
Own special way

*Coleen Bradshaw*

## ENGLAND...

England not a place for bicycles,
Not too fast and not too slow,
Violence and murder all around,
But we don't want to know,
We turn our backs,
We close our eyes,
National pride died long.

Never to be a superpower,
But always rubbing shoulders,
Happy sending arms to others,
Then we're sending soldiers,
Divide and rule,
Britain was so cool,
But now resentment smoulders.

The pretty English public parks,
Are now bereft of flowers,
Visited by the unemployed,
Who sit around for hours,
They dream of the Times,
On the breakfast table,
As if prisoners in towers.

The emotions of a nation lie,
In tatters after eighteen years,
We British did so well to hold,
Back the frustrations and the fears,
The smart abused,
The ignorant confused,
That's why the Tories left to jeers.

*Dilip Datta*

## THE SKIVER

Once when I got out of bed
I felt like skiving instead
I sat by the loo, pretending to spew
It was school that I seemed to most dread
My mum didn't believe me at first
She should have expected the worst
She looked at the floor with a disgusted face
And I knew that my trick had worked
Later that day when my mum went out
I decided to venture about
I looked in the cupboard and saw mum's mistake
For there on the shelf was jelly and cake
The very next day I didn't have to fake a spew
I ended up spending a day in the loo
In the school I found myself
All thanks to jelly on the shelf . . .

*Chris Adamson (12)*


## OFF WITH HIS HEAD

'The simplest way' the doctor said:
'Is to remove the patient's head,
He's got nothing much on top
He'll not miss a cranial crop.'

The patient said: 'I'll mean no harm,
But with my head beneath my arm
On gloomy evenings, surgery night,
Patients will face a fearsome sight.'

'They'll say: Not stupid. After all
At least he knows the place to call!'
Try therapy, at any rate,
Before you start to amputate.'

*John Urwin*

## BORN FOR BETTER

Hunters Warriors aye even Kings
We were once all these things
Roaming free over our own domain
Always proud never knowing shame

Came the intruders to our land
Slaughtering at will, our once proud land
Some they did not kill, the unlucky ones
Taken from their wives and sons.

Transported to very distant lands
Bound and shackled in iron bands
I'll feel, unwashed day after day
In our own muck we were made to lay

Still shackled then finally caged
Heads unbrushed still we raged
That this could be our fate
Homeless, without friend or mate

Then more strangers came and stared
Friends of the invaders, maybe, who cares
Not I, for I am well prepared to die
Rather than suffer in this misery

Dreams of home came more and more often
But these wondrous thoughts cannot soften
The ache of wanting once more to roam
Those wondrous glorious fields of home

Alas this will never be,
The once proud beast which was me
Is gone and will never more
Give freely my unbounded roar.

**R Middleton**

## THE WOMAN ALONE

She'd phoned Emily and phoned Paul
Giggled with Marion over the wall,
Called on her neighbour, who wasn't well
And then returned to her private hell.
She'd checked the gas bill, electric too,
Stood too long in the supermarket queue:
Exclaimed at the prices of goods they sell
And then returned to her private hell.
She turned out old clothes she wanted to sort,
Then made lunch from the things she'd bought,
Watered the garden as twilight fell -
And then re-entered her private hell.

Who would have thought, seeing her smile,
She'd ever be lonely once in a while?
No-one saw tears so no-one could tell
What it was like in her private hell.

She made herself cook her dinner for one;
Realised summer had almost gone,
Heard the doom-ridden Passing Bell -
And then looked round at her private hell.
She awoke, at dawn, to clear blue skies,
To sunshine that made her blink her eyes
She washed and dressed, determined to repel
The thought of her silent private hell:
So she phoned Emily and phoned Paul
Spoke to Marion over the wall,
Called on her neighbour who wasn't well -
But still she crept back to her private hell.

***Dorothy Thompson***

## INFORMATION

We hope you have enjoyed reading this book - and that you will continue to enjoy it in the coming years.

If you like reading and writing poetry drop us a line, or give us a call, and we'll send you a free information pack.

Write to :-
**Anchor Books Information
1-2 Wainman Road
Woodston
Peterborough
PE2 7BU
(01733) 230761**